Cross Country Skiing

Cross Country Skiing

WITHDRAWN

Ronald Crawford-Currie

VNR **VAN NOSTRAND REINHOLD COMPANY**

NEW YORK   CINCINNATI   TORONTO   LONDON   MELBOURNE

Library of Congress Catalog Card Number: 82-8620

ISBN 0-442-21512-6

Published in the United States in 1982 by Van Nostrand Reinhold Company Inc., 135 West 50th Street, New York, NY 10020, U.S.A.

Van Nostrand Reinhold Publishing, 1410 Birchmount Road, Scarborough, Ontario M1P 2E7, Canada

Van Nostrand Reinhold Australia Pty. Ltd., 17 Queen Street, Mitcham, Victoria 3132, Australia

Van Nostrand Reinhold Company Limited, Molly Millars Lane, Wokingham, Berkshire, England

16 15 14 13 12 11 10 9 8 7 6 5 4 3 2 1

Library of Congress Cataloging in Publication Data

Crawford-Currie, Ronald.
  Cross-country skiing.

  Bibliography: p. 155.
  Includes index.
  1. Cross-country skiing. I. Title.
GV855.3.C7 1982 796.93 82-8620
ISBN 0-442-21512-6   AACR2

CROSS-COUNTRY SKIING has been originated and produced by AB Nordbok, Gothenburg, Sweden, in close collaboration with the author and an international team of experts and photographers.

Editor-in-Chief: Turlough Johnston.
Editor: Jon van Leuven.
Graphical and color design: Lars Jödahl.

Most of the drawings have been made by Ulf Söderqvist. The drawn sequences of skiing and training are based on photographs taken by Fritz Solvang and Michael Brady. Other drawings have been made by Anders Engström (pages 44–45, 46, 138–139), Lennart Molin (page 118b), and Yusuke Nagano (pages 32–33). The paintings were made by Thomas Wallden and Syed Mumtaz Ahmad.

Photographs: Aftenposten (page 147), Bergans/Ørnelund AS (page 38), Michael Brady (pages 46–47), Åke Hedlund (jacket front, pages 66, 110–111, 142), Curt Kempe (pages 130–131), Inge Persson (pages 150–151), Galen Rowell (jacket back, pages 7, 138), Peter Skoghagen (pages 78, 90), Helge Sunde (pages 2–3, 27, 54, 82, 94–95, 114, 126, 134), Theo van Houts (pages 86–87).

Lithographics: Nils Hermansson.

CONTENTS

Preface 6

1 Fitness 7

2 Equipment 27

3 Technique 55

4 Touring 83

5 Orienteering 115

6 Safety 127

7 Famous races 143

Bibliography 155

Index 156

PREFACE

Skiing through the winter countryside has evolved for many thousands of years, from a means of travel and hunting to a specialized kind of sport and recreation. Archaeological discoveries prove that skis were used by about 2500 BC in Scandinavia, whose mythology had a god and goddess of skiing, and there are old rock carvings in northern Europe which display skiers. The word "ski" itself is of Germanic origin and once meant a long split piece of wood. The early adoption of skis by nomadic peoples in these regions is exemplified by the Lapps. They appear in drawings made a few centuries ago by visitors from the south, showing strange folk who glided across the snowy wastes on long wooden objects. At the end of the last century, Lapps astonished the world with their ability to travel far and fast on skis. By contrast, skis were evidently unknown until recently in the Himalaya area, despite its cold winters and difficult terrain, and skis only reached North America with immigrants as from Norway.

Today, it is especially in central Europe and North America that the tradition of cross-country skiing and touring has grown into one of the most popular leisure activities of the winter season. This is largely because of a reaction against our increasing dependence on the advanced technology and great specialization in modern society. Through our deeper concern with meaningful free time, particularly as outdoor activity, we are making a conscious or unconscious effort to regain contact with the ways of life that were closer to nature in previous generations. Unfortunately, many of us try to deal with the problems of skiing in the same complicated manner as we solve those of society. But improved techniques and devices still have only a limited value when we are faced with the huge forces of nature. Rather than controlling the environment, a skier must adapt to it, and this is best done by combining the experience of past peoples with the new methods of our time.

The following pages contain much technical and practical advice on choosing equipment and how to use it properly for various ski tours. Once you have made an honest assessment of your potential as a skier, the amount of skiing you expect to do, and where you will mainly do it, this fundamental knowledge should prepare you well for enjoyable touring. A far more difficult task would be to convey the actual satisfactions and skills which can only be absorbed with repeated tours under diverse conditions. These you must find out for yourself. There are no short cuts to good skiing and familiarity with extreme environments such as high mountain terrain in winter. Only continued training and a growing awareness of the surroundings will enable you to decide what you can and want to do. Never let ski touring become longer or harder than your abilities and pleasure allow. You are the source of your own experience.

This book about cross-country skiing and open-air living is dedicated to my sons John and Peter.

Ronald Crawford-Currie
June 1982

Fitness 1

Over a very long period of time, the human body has adapted itself to ways of life in which hard work was an important component. But another result of the body's evolution is its ability to deal with a great variety of demands. One of these is adjustment to a low level of physical effort, as in the modern world which surrounds us with technological aids that make labor unnecessary. Because of assistance by machines, electronic computers, new methods of transport and communication, and so on, we now have more leisure than ever before. And since our innate curiosity continues, seeking fresh experiences and even real adventures, there is an increased need for the meaningful use of leisure. Many leisure activities today are related to the customs of earlier generations and to the countryside near which we live or which we can reach in our free time. Cross-country skiing is a leading example.

Forested areas and upland regions with mountains may be fairly inaccessible during large parts of the year. But when the ground freezes, ice covers the watercourses, and enough snow has fallen, such places become appreciably easier to move about in. In order to discover this at first hand, you must have some skill on skis, the right equipment, and a certain degree of fitness.

Much of the satisfaction derived from a new experience comes from the planning and preparation that should precede it. An expedition team aiming to climb a mountain in winter, a group setting out to tour on skis for several days with overnight stops at cabins, or just a few people skiing down a forest trail—all ought to look ahead and get ready. Reaching the objectives will make different demands on each individual, but what remains true for everyone is that, the better their physical fitness, the easier it becomes to achieve the chosen goal. Besides, being in good condition means that the margin of safety is improved when risks must be taken.

An important way of preparing yourself is to accustom the body to increased effort—in other words, to train. Most people think of training as something especially for top-ranking sportsmen. That is not true. This chapter will explain why training is essential also for the ordinary skier, and how you can devise a training schedule which is suited to you and to your ambitions as a skier. It is not enough to know that you should train: you need further motivation to get started properly and, above all, to continue on a regular basis.

Energy-producing processes

Forty per cent of your body weight is due to muscles. They are attached to the skeleton by tendons, and the various joints are usually provided with ligaments. The skeleton itself may be described as a system of levers which are worked by muscles. To do this, the muscles contract—their long fine fibers become shorter. Muscles are powered by the release of chemically bound energy which is transformed into the energy of movement as well as some heat. The process may begin with a signal from the brain to the central nervous system, or with a direct reflex that normally comes from the spinal cord. The central nervous system controls all communications in the body, receiving and analyzing signals, and sending orders to diverse muscles. Some of these orders are carried out voluntarily—for instance, the conscious actions of jumping or swimming—even if the movement is executed automatically. Others, such as the heart's beating or the rhythm of breathing, are completely involuntary.

The function of body muscles can be compared with what happens in an internal-combustion engine. The body obtains fuel from a supply of food, mainly from the fat and sugar in it. An "ignition" source is the central nervous system, and an "exhaust" is the removal of waste products and other residues by the blood. The energy-releasing chemical reaction in muscles operates best if oxygen is available to the muscles. More exactly, physiologists distinguish between two kinds of energy-releasing processes. In one process, called aerobic ("with air"), energy-rich substances are burned with the aid of oxygen. In the other, termed anaerobic ("without air"), such substances are broken down directly without oxygen. The human body makes use of both these processes, as will be described below.

Scientific research on both top-class and ordinary sportsmen has shown that the chief limitation to an individual's performance of a physical task involves the capacity to supply the working muscles with oxygen. The decisive factor here is not the quantity of energy-producing substances, so what determines the availability of oxygen in a muscle? Oxygen forms about twenty-one per cent of the air around us and is absorbed through tiny sacs called alveoli in the lungs, where it combines with the blood's red pigment, called haemoglobin. The heart pumps this oxygenated blood throughout the

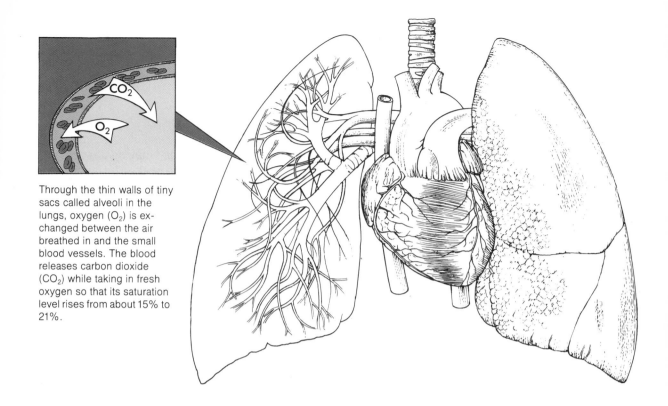

Through the thin walls of tiny sacs called alveoli in the lungs, oxygen (O_2) is exchanged between the air breathed in and the small blood vessels. The blood releases carbon dioxide (CO_2) while taking in fresh oxygen so that its saturation level rises from about 15% to 21%.

body, from the large arteries to the fine capillaries which supply the smallest muscle tissues. After delivering its oxygen, the blood carries away the waste products from the combustion process, so that these reach the right places for purification and disposal: for example, in the kidneys, or in the lungs when carbon dioxide is expelled by breathing. The blood is once again oxygenated in the lungs, circulates through the body, releases oxygen, and collects waste products, continuing the cycle.

If the body is at rest or is exerting itself only moderately, this cycle goes on with no great strain upon any of its stages. However, when the degree of physical exertion increases, the body has to adapt, firstly by increasing the amount of air that passes through the lungs, and secondly by speeding up the blood circulation. Greater exertion is indicated by breathlessness and a faster heartbeat. After a few minutes, stable conditions are achieved, even if the exertion is still increasing. Your lungs operate more powerfully, you breathe more rapidly and deeply, and your heart pumps harder in order to send sufficient blood around the body. The amount of blood leaving the heart every minute varies widely, from 4–6 liters (7–10 pints) during moderate physical effort, to 25–35 liters (44–62 pints) during strenuous exertion as in competitive cross-country skiing.

Thus, it is the state of training of the circulatory apparatus—lungs, heart, and blood vessels—and its work capacity that determines what is generally called fitness. Most people can improve their fitness by suitable training, so that the body becomes accustomed to working harder by progressively increasing the load placed upon it. The important thing is that you should regard your training as something enjoyable and meaningful, not unpleasant and boring. Regular training will not only equip you to go skiing without getting exhausted, but also produce a physical sense of well-being that will enhance your daily life.

Using oxygen

There is an inherent sluggishness in the body's system which makes it unable to utilize the process of aerobic combustion immediately when its work load is increased. To cope with a sudden concentrated effort, such as a fifty-yard sprint or a powerful jump, the muscles depend upon anaerobic combustion, like an auxiliary engine, releasing energy without using oxygen. This process can serve only for a short, intensive effort, as its fuel is available in limited amounts, and because it forms a waste product called lactic acid. Too much lactic acid in a muscle acts as a poison. The muscle no longer works satisfactorily but feels dead and reacts more slowly, or not at all, to nerve impulses.

When the body is at rest, the
pulse is around 70 beats per
minute and the heart pumps
out some 5 liters (10 pints) of
blood each minute. Every
liter of venous blood takes up
50 milliliters (3 cubic inches)
of oxygen when passing
through the lungs, so a
total of 250 ml per minute is
used. The arterial blood
under normal conditions is
saturated with oxygen and
contains around 200 ml per
liter.

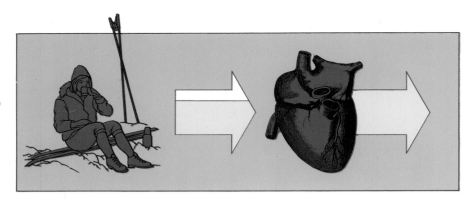

Even with moderate work,
the pulse rises to about 90
beats per minute and the
heart's ability to pump out
blood is utilized more fully.
The blood is oxygenated
more effectively and takes up
100 ml per liter per minute.
Activity then requires an oxygen consumption of 1 liter
per minute.

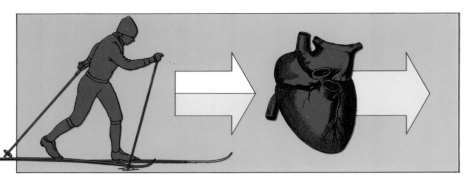

With hard effort, the heart's
capacity must be used to the
maximum, pumping as much
blood as possible with each
beat, at a pulse of around
180 per minute. Some 20
liters of blood then leave the
heart each minute, taking up
150 ml of oxygen per liter, in
order to supply the 3 liters of
oxygen needed for such
work.

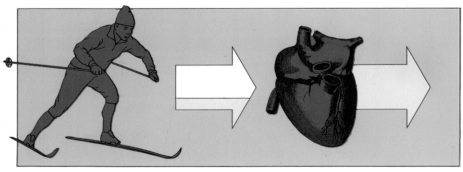

Lactic acid has to be transported away from the
muscle by the blood and is broken down with the
aid of oxygen. It is then transformed into new energy-rich compounds in the liver and elsewhere. But
these changes need some time, and the anaerobic
process is restricted to the moments when the
physical effort begins. After one or two minutes, the
lungs and heart become adapted so that the aerobic process takes over. If the work load is suddenly
increased again or is greater than the maximum
which an individual can cope with, the anaerobic
process can once more be utilized briefly until it is
stopped by exhaustion.

Your fitness may be measured in various ways.
One method is to measure how much oxygen you
can absorb from the air in a minute. Normally, body
weight must be taken into account, as a load that
requires energy to be moved. A heavy body demands more energy than a lighter one, so the capacity to use oxygen is expressed in terms of oxygen
volume per body weight (as in milliliters per kilogram) per minute. The highest values of oxygen
absorption have been measured for top-class long-
distance skiers: 85—90 ml/kg-min, compared
with the normal 30—40 ml/kg-min for less active
adults.

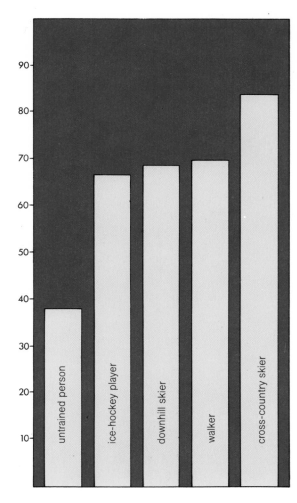

90-
80-
70-
60-
50-
40-
30-
20-
10-

untrained person | ice-hockey player | downhill skier | walker | cross-country skier

The individual's ability to take up oxygen and transport it to the muscles determines his or her working capacity. Here, a healthy but untrained person is compared with sportsmen in various fields as regards maximum oxygen intake, which is measured in milliliters per kilogram per minute.

always produces a higher capacity and increased physical well-being, regardless of sex or age.

The muscles

Each muscle in your body consists of numerous fibers, arranged in groups and functioning together as a unit. These fibers have the ability to contract by reducing their length, or to be tensed for withstanding the forces exerted on them. There are two main types of musculature in the body. One type, smooth muscle, surrounds many of the inner organs, and its action is involuntary. The other type is called striped, striated, or skeletal muscle, and we usually refer to this when speaking of muscles.

A group of muscles is controlled by a nerve cell in the spinal cord, through a nerve fiber that branches to reach the individual muscle fibers and stimulate them simultaneously, so that they act together as a "motor unit". The striped muscles also contain a sensory organ, sometimes called a muscle spindle or a stretch receptor, which informs the central nervous system about how much or how little the muscle fibers contract or stretch. Messages from all these groups of fibers give the nervous system a "picture" of the work load on the various muscles, and also of the relative positions of the parts of the body.

Closer study of the fibers in striped muscle reveals that they are of two kinds, red and white. Both are found in every individual, with the interesting feature that the ratio of their amounts may vary from person to person. The red fibers are slightly slower in contracting and can work for longer periods, while the white fibers contract more quickly and powerfully. Exercise that continues for a long time, such as a skiing tour, puts a heavy demand on the red fibers. In practice, therefore, the proportion of "fast" to "slow" fibers will partly determine whether the individual is suited to short efforts or to tasks that demand more stamina.

Muscles often operate across joints of the skeleton. In order to be able to bend a limb as well as to extend it, one must have different muscles for the two functions. When one muscle contracts to bend the limb, other muscles must stretch, so that they can subsequently contract and return the limb to its normal position. In this way, because muscles work in opposition, they also fulfill the purpose of preventing exaggerated movements, which might go as far as to damage the operation of a muscle.

In reality, most of the movements executed by a person are so complex that many distinct muscles and muscle groups act at once, directed by the central nervous system—the brain, spinal cord,

Some difference exists between men and women in this respect, even when the lower average weight of women is allowed for. Research has shown that women rate twenty to thirty per cent lower than men of the same age and in about the same degree of training. Age is another factor that affects fitness, by decreasing the work capacity of the heart and the elasticity of the blood vessels. It is usually reckoned that an individual has the greatest stamina—capacity for physical exertion over a relatively long period—between the ages of twenty-five and thirty-five. But there is obviously great variation between individuals, and regular exercise

The skeletal musculature has various fibers organized in bundles consisting of thousands of long thin cells. Among them are the fibrils which enable muscles to contract.

In sports which demand great stamina, the participant needs a high ratio of slow muscle fibers with much endurance. Shown here is the percentage of such fibers in the thigh muscles of top sportsmen in several fields. These are also called red fibers and are surrounded by a dense net of capillaries. Their cells contain many mitochondria which give a large capacity for using energy.

nerve cells, and nerve fibers. Harmonious combination of all these muscle contractions, to produce a movement or a sequence of movements, is what we mean by coordination. This is of special significance when an activity involving technique and skill, such as skiing, is concerned. If your technique is correct, the result will be that your muscles do not have to work as hard as those of a less proficient skier.

Physiological research has also demonstrated that a working muscle requires a continuous supply of oxygen in order to be able to go on contracting. If a muscle alternately contracts and relaxes, this "pumping" action produces better circulation of the blood than in a muscle which remains tensed for a long time or has only short intervals of rest. The difference between a well-trained skier with correct techniques and a less trained, occasional skier may be that the former allows short periods of rest to the muscles between powerful bursts of exertion, whereas the latter's muscles stay tensed. Thus, the efficient skier enjoys not only a higher oxygen intake and better condition, but also more power from internal sources, like an engine that does not need to be pushed so close to its maximum output and can employ an economical cruising gear.

Of the two different ways in which muscles work, one is called isotonic, meaning that the tension of a muscle remains constant although it contracts as the fibers shorten. But if the length does not change while the fibers are tensed, isometric work is done. Both kinds of work can occur either in long, sustained effort or in brief, intense bursts. In long-distance skiing, the body is primarily subject to sustained, isotonic contractions of the muscles, rather than to bearing extreme loads for very short times.

How to tackle your training

If your body has grown unaccustomed to exercise during a couple of years or more, you will now be considerably out of condition, perhaps without having even noticed it. All the organs of your body will have undergone a gradual deterioration, which you may have felt only by finding yourself out of breath after taking a short walk or climbing stairs. To get the maximum benefit and enjoyment from skiing, you should gradually and purposefully build up your fitness again, just as you gradually let it go.

Once you start to train, the positive aspect of your lack of fitness is that you will soon see an improvement. But it is essential that regular training continues. Experiments have shown that a suitable training schedule consists of two or three sessions a week. Each period should last from thirty to forty-five minutes. To this you must add time for reaching and leaving the training area or gymnasium, ten to fifteen minutes for warming-up exercises, and time for showering and dressing after the session. If you make up your mind to set aside two periods, each of ninety minutes, from the total of 168 hours in a week, you will quickly begin to feel better and achieve more.

Some people like to train in the morning, before going to work, and others prefer the afternoon or evening. It makes no difference which you choose—the vital point is to train regularly and with determination. After a time, training will become as much a part of your routine as eating, washing, or going to bed. When this has happened, you will not think of avoiding or giving up your training, because you would feel that something was missing.

If it has been a long time since you were physically active, you should begin very gently and carefully, but regularly two or three times a week. When in doubt, consult someone who can advise you on organizing your training program. Walking, cycling, and swimming are examples of good activities for building fitness. Try to train in the company of people whom you know or who have the same interest, as this is always easier and more pleasant. There are modern centers with facilities for group exercise where allowance can be made for the initial condition of different individuals. Before long, you will find that you can walk farther and faster, cycle better, and swim with less strain.

It must be emphasized that time is needed for building up fitness, particularly to enable the organs that carry oxygen in the body to adapt to greater loads. A proper training program should extend over as much as two years. However, if you start to train in late summer or early fall, you will experience a considerable improvement in condition by the winter season.

Implicit in all training, of course, is some development of your general muscular strength. It has been shown that the training of a muscle group leads relatively quickly—within a few months—to an appreciable gain in strength. Long-distance skiing and ski touring do not place exceptional demands on muscular strength and, to a great extent, the same muscle groups are used in skiing as in walking or running. Nevertheless, it may be useful to do some extra work on the arms and shoulders, as you exercise these a good deal in using ski poles. General training of the whole body, with concentration on the corset of muscles around the stomach and back, together with exercises to improve agility and suppleness, should be a permanent feature of the program.

Time will also be needed in building up and strengthening the tendons, ligaments, and cartilages of your limbs, if you have been inactive for a large part of your life. Ligaments and tendons are less well endowed with blood vessels than, for example, muscle tissues, and this makes their strengthening and development more difficult when the load imposed on them is increased by a regular training program. Elasticity also decreases with age, and a damaged ligament or tendon takes a long time to recover fully. There is every reason,

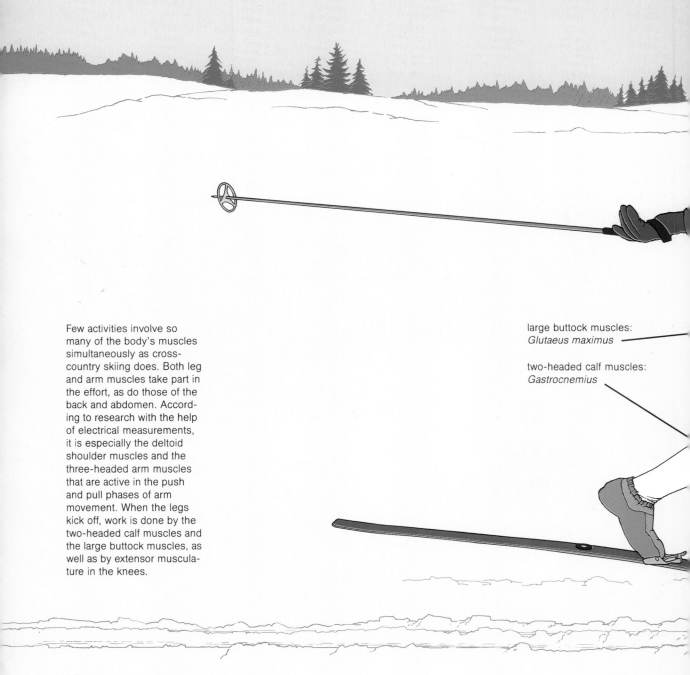

Few activities involve so many of the body's muscles simultaneously as cross-country skiing does. Both leg and arm muscles take part in the effort, as do those of the back and abdomen. According to research with the help of electrical measurements, it is especially the deltoid shoulder muscles and the three-headed arm muscles that are active in the push and pull phases of arm movement. When the legs kick off, work is done by the two-headed calf muscles and the large buttock muscles, as well as by extensor musculature in the knees.

large buttock muscles:
Glutaeus maximus

two-headed calf muscles:
Gastrocnemius

then, to begin carefully and increase your exertions gradually. The capacity of the body to produce synovial fluid for lubrication in the active joints, tendons, and ligaments will also require a certain amount of time, before it is developed satisfactorily.

All physical activities should be preceded by warming-up exercises that involve the whole body. Their purpose is to enable the body to gear itself for the coming exertion. They increase the circulation of blood in the working muscles and release the energy-rich substances that fuel the chemical processes which are necessary in carrying out the desired movements. Warming up will also raise the body temperature to the level where these processes can occur with maximum speed and efficiency. You should spend around fifteen minutes warming up, with exercise for all the muscle groups that will be brought into action by the activity.

delta muscles: *Deltoideus*

three-headed arm muscles: *Triceps brachii*

extensor musculature in knee joint: *Rectus femoris, Vastus lateralis*

Food

The food we eat every day gives us the fuel necessary to sustain the various organs of the body and to enable us to move about. Our food consists principally of proteins, fats, and carbohydrates. In addition, we need substances such as minerals and vitamins. All these are found to a greater or lesser extent in our daily meals. Today, of course, we often eat more food, and with different components, than was usual when daily work demanded great physical effort. In modern western society, where the need for exertion is constantly being reduced, we have not always adapted to smaller requirements of energy by eating less food. The result has been that many people are overweight—a problem of affluence.

It is reckoned that a lumberjack requires an energy intake of 5,000−6,000 calories per day to do his work, whereas someone with a sedentary job in an office needs no more than 2,000 calories per day. A good day's skiing, while carrying packs over terrain with perhaps substantial differences in height, may demand an energy intake of 8,000−10,000 calories. These examples show clearly that there is a relationship between the work to be performed and the amount of energy required. Thus, it is advisable to adjust the quantity of food you eat to the physical effort you will be making.

In practical terms, this means that if you have been inactive lately and have grown accustomed to eating less, you must now increase your intake of food to meet the demands of ski touring. However, if you are overweight, you need to do two things: get your weight down as part of your training, and ensure that you eat enough of the right kinds of food for physical activity. Obviously, therefore, it would not be wise to lose weight by starving yourself on your skiing trips. Losing weight, like fitness training, should take place gradually over a period of time. On the other hand, moving a heavy body around will always demand more effort and energy than is needed for a lighter body. A surplus weight of 12−15 kg (26−33 lb) is not unusual for many people today, but one can hardly imagine perpetually carrying such a heavy rucksack about.

The proteins in our food are the body's building materials, needed to construct and replace the cells, which require constant renewal. The energy used by muscles for their work comes mainly from the burning of fats and carbohydrates. These two energy-rich materials have somewhat different characteristics and are employed by the body in different ways. The fat that we do not expend in physical activity is stored as fat tissue, while the carbohydrates that we do not burn up can be stored by the body to only a limited extent. One may compare fats with a low-octane fuel, and carbohydrates with a high-octane fuel. In light or moderate physical activity, the body burns both of them in roughly equal proportions. For a greater work load and degree of effort, the muscles tend to prefer carbohydrates as fuel. Whereas the body can utilize its quantities of stored fat over a period of days or even weeks, stored carbohydrates are available for just a few hours of work.

Carbohydrates take the form of glycogen in the muscles, a larger reserve of glycogen in the liver, and sugar in the blood. Since the muscles use carbohydrates almost exclusively when providing energy for hard physical exertion and only a limited amount can be stored, you must make sure to replenish the supply throughout your longer ski tours. If you use up your reserve of glycogen, it will need one or two days to be restored. This is one reason why a day of strenuous effort, covering a great distance or hilly terrain, should be followed by a day of rest or a fairly short journey. Similarly, you should judge whether you need a large carbohydrate intake before and after a session of hard training, to replace what you have burned up.

Another important point is that the central nervous system can function only by means of carbohydrate combustion. Consequently, when the availability of carbohydrates in the body is reduced, the demands of the central nervous system take priority. The muscles will then have to make do with using up fat, resulting in a lower level of activity.

Drink

In order to function properly, the body needs a certain amount of fluids as well as its daily food requirement. One role of fluids is connected with the regulation of heat: the body must rid itself of the excess heat which is always produced by hard exercise. When food is consumed, about eighty percent of its chemically bound energy is con-

In all training, it is important to try to imitate the proper movements as closely as possible. Choose any smooth uphill slope about 200–300 m (650–1,000 ft) long. Walk up it with long steps, using your poles. Get a feeling of how to glide upward, and move your foot far forward with each step. To make a high demand on the circulatory system, you must work in intervals of at least 2–3 minutes. You will be practicing diagonal movement and at the same time training the elasticity and strength of your arms and legs.

When the ground is bare of snow and you are preparing for winter, it is advantageous to practice on roller-skis as a complement to other training. The pattern of movements is similar to that of cross-country skiing and is best done as long-distance training. You must have already acquired good skiing habits and correct technique. Moving on roller-skis will give excellent training for arms, legs, and the upper body. You can practice both the diagonal stride and poling.

Exercises which tend to
strengthen different muscles
as well as increasing the
body's mobility.

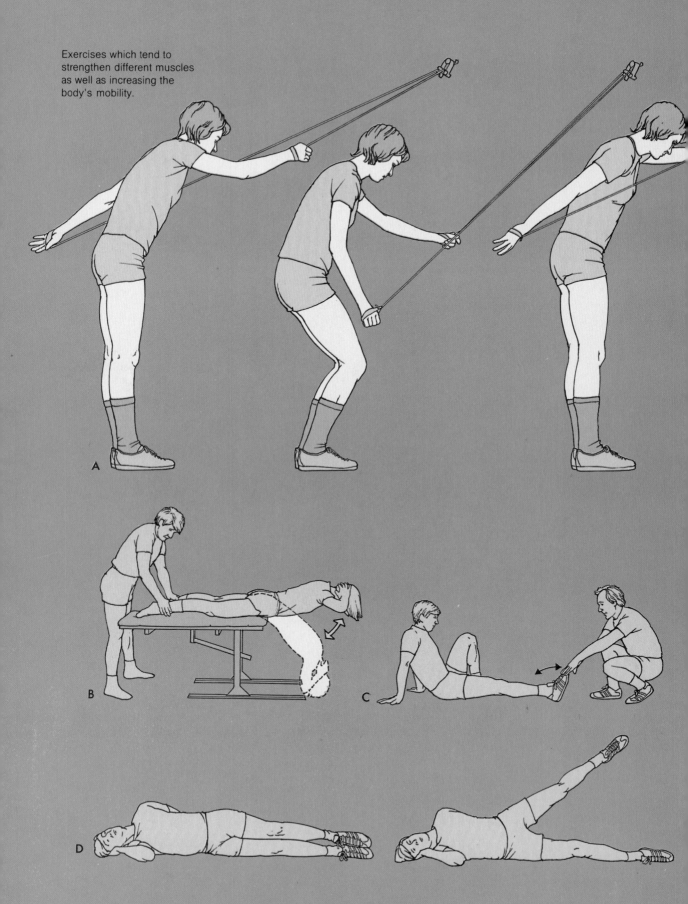

A

B

C

D

A With the help of elastic bands fastened to the wall, you can train the diagonal working of your arms. Stand far enough away from the wall to enable you to pull regularly from the beginning. Work rhythmically and with light yielding of the knees.

B Training of the back by raising and lowering the upper body. The effort can be varied if you hold your hands out to the sides, near the neck, or stretched above your head.

C Training of the front lower leg muscles which lift up the foot and are especially strained in downhill skiing. Sit on the floor and try to raise the foot against the opposing force. Train both legs equally well.

D Lie on your side and lift the straight upper leg, upward and somewhat backward. You should not lean your pelvis in any direction but must work only with the hip muscles. Do the exercise with both legs an equal number of times.

E Sitting up to train the straight abdominal muscles. Lie on your back with hands folded behind your head and both legs bent. Raise yourself from the floor but keep the small of your back on the floor.

F Training the oblique abdominal muscles. Lie on your back with bent legs and both arms stretched out to one side. Lift your upper body and turn it to the side at the same time. Return slowly to the initial position. Exercise to both left and right.

G Push-ups to train the arms and shoulders.

H Lie on your back with bent legs and the arms along the sides. Press the hip region slowly upward until only the shoulders and feet are in contact with the ground. Sink slowly back down. This trains the buttock muscles and back.

I Stand on one leg, and bend and stretch the same leg as many times as you can. Do not go too far down. Train both legs. This exercise strengthens the legs and also trains your balance.

19

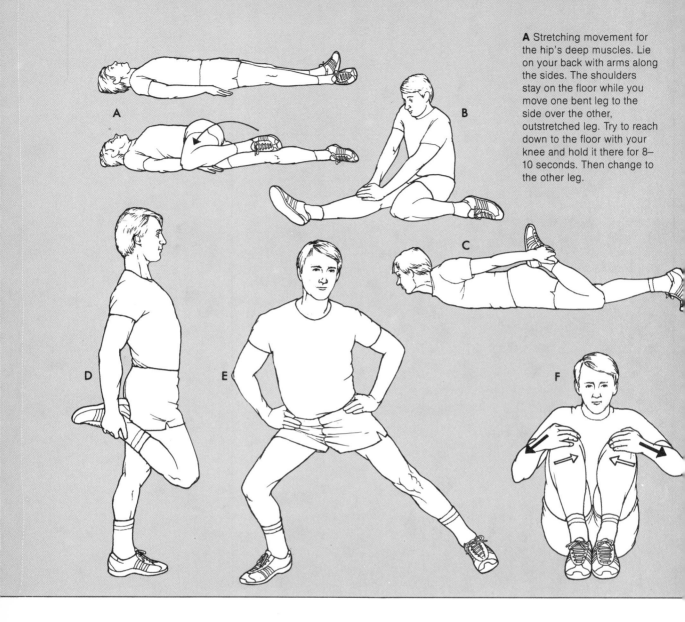

A Stretching movement for the hip's deep muscles. Lie on your back with arms along the sides. The shoulders stay on the floor while you move one bent leg to the side over the other, outstretched leg. Try to reach down to the floor with your knee and hold it there for 8–10 seconds. Then change to the other leg.

B Sit with one leg stretched in front of you and the other bent to the side and backward. Bend yourself forward and press the front knee with your hands for 8–10 seconds. This movement stretches the muscles at the back of the leg.

C Lie on your stomach and bend one leg. Hold your ankle with the hand on the same side and press your heel against your buttock for as long as you can. Do not make any violent movements, but softly stretch out the front thigh muscles.

D The thigh muscles can also be stretched in a standing position. Hold your ankle with both hands and press the heel against the buttock. At the same time, push your hips forward and try to extend the thigh muscles so that the knee points straight down.

verted into heat, leaving approximately twenty percent for direct conversion into muscular work. If the work rate is low and the environment is cool, you do not have to lose much heat. But if the work rate or the temperature is increased, large quantities of fluid evaporate in the form of sweat, removing heat and cooling you down.

A fluid loss of two to three per cent of your body weight represents about 1.5 to 2 liters (2.5 to 3.5 pints) of water. This reduces your efficiency by more than twenty per cent, if you weigh around 75 kg (165 lb). In very hard physical exertion, you lose up to 2 liters (3.5 pints) of fluid per hour. Having something to drink at regular intervals is essential when you are skiing, whether on a practice run or on a long and strenuous tour.

E Stretching exercise for the inner thigh and groin. Let the foot and the bent leg point in the same direction. Bend and stretch the leg alternately so that you feel the muscles extending regularly.

Make no jerky movements, and do not go down too deeply in the knee joint. Bend it by 90° at most.
F Sit on the floor with bent legs. Hold the hands around the knees and try to pull them apart. Resist this force for 8–10 seconds in order to train the inward-turning leg muscles.
G Stretching exercises for the back. Backward stretches with the left and right legs forward alternately. Soft stretching ten times for each leg. Make slow stretching movements from side to side with the arms along the sides or extended over the head.

H Hang by the hands and swing the whole body sideways in a relaxed manner so as to strengthen the arms, shoulders, and side muscles of the trunk and hips.

I Stretching of back muscles by alternately hunching and swaying with the back. The initial position is on hands and knees with slightly bent elbows, eyes to the floor, and straight neck and back.

J Lie on your back with arms along your sides. Lift the legs up and lower them back over the head. Reach as far back as possible with the tips of your toes.

All these exercises both strengthen and extend the muscles. Every stretching should be performed calmly and methodically without violent movements. Warm up in the normal way before you begin the exercises.

In spite of the fact that what you are skiing on is frozen water, it can be difficult to obtain sufficient drinking water when you are out in the woods or in a wilderness area in winter. A lot of time and fuel is needed to melt enough snow for your requirements, so you should be sure to drink enough liquid when you stop for a meal and have to melt snow for your cooking in any case. During the day, you should carry warm drinks with you, preferably containing a little sugar to provide additional carbohydrate. Use Thermos flasks, or allow time to boil up something drinkable when stopping for food. On practice runs, it is enough to have some drink with you and take about 1/4 liter (1/2 pint) after thirty or forty minutes of skiing, depending on how hard and fast you have been going.

Problems of cold

In our discussion of training and diet, we have seen that the chemical processes in the body function best at a certain temperature, and that a large part of the energy released has to be removed in the form of excess heat. It follows that the best way of keeping warm in winter, in addition to wearing the right kind of clothing, is to be physically active. As the body constantly loses heat to the surrounding cold air, the loss must be balanced by heat produced in muscular work.

Living organisms have the tendency to adopt a low level of activity in cold conditions, decreasing their rate of metabolism when the external temperature drops. The body's first reaction is to cut off the blood supply to the outer skin layers, and to concentrate on the more vital organs and the working muscles. If the internal temperature, normally about 37°C (98.6°F), drops towards 34°C (93°F), the person lapses into apathy and must receive assistance from his companions to prevent further loss of body heat. At 32°C (90°F), he loses consciousness—and if his temperature falls below 30°C (86°F), the heart begins to labor and dangerous convulsions may develop. If the body in this condition has already nearly exhausted its store of carbohydrate through earlier exertions, the chances of any vital energy combustion occurring now are reduced further.

Your clothes should be chosen to keep you warm as well as leaving great freedom of movement.

23

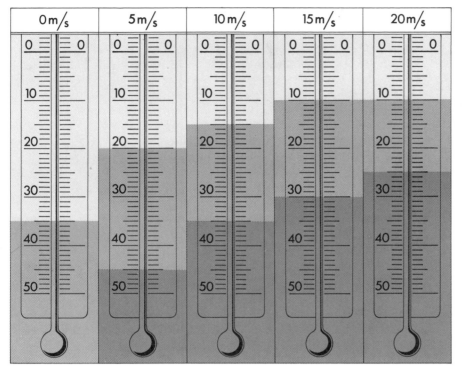

0 m/s	5 m/s	10 m/s	15 m/s	20 m/s

The danger of frostbite increases with the wind speed. For example, when it is calm, there is little risk of frostbite down to −35°C (−31°F) but, at 5 meters per second (16 ft/s), the danger exists below −20°C (−4°F).

Wind speed can be judged as follows. When it is calm, smoke will rise straight up from a chimney. At 5 m/s, the smoke is blown gently away. At 10 m/s, thin branches begin to shake. At 15 m/s, whole trees will sway. At 20 m/s, branches are broken by the wind.

Risk of frostbite:

☐ insignificant risk

▨ increased risk

▧ major risk

It is important to remember that the brain needs a continuous supply of large quantities of oxygen-rich warm blood in order to function, and the body cannot afford any "savings" here. If the temperature of the brain drops by only a few tenths of a degree Centigrade, its efficiency decreases, thus affecting its capacity to receive nerve impulses, process them, and give the necessary orders to the muscles for carrying out appropriate actions. The capacity for logical deduction diminishes and an increasing paralysis of action sets in. A normally dressed person loses up to fifty percent of surplus heat through the head, so we should not aim to "keep a cool head" in these circumstances.

Guarding the body against unwanted heat loss means wearing proper clothing and protecting the "freezing points"—the head, neck, wrists, waist, abdomen, knees, and ankles. It also means special protection for all the places where large blood vessels are near the surface and exposed to cooling. If freezing continues in spite of such protection, the body will first guard the internal organs and the central nervous system, notably the brain. The result may be that the blood supply to the extremities is cut off to an extent so great that frostbite occurs, as on the tip of the nose, the cheeks, ears

and, after excessive cooling, the fingers and toes.

Frostbite exists when the fluid in the cells is changed to ice crystals and the cells cease their vital function. If the frostbite is superficial and does not last long, it is fairly easy to thaw the frozen area. Usually, one can raise one's body temperature sufficiently by taking shelter, putting on more clothing, consuming hot food and drink, and possibly increasing activity. However, if the freezing has been more drastic and has gone deeper into the body tissues, the cells may die and the frostbitten person then requires special treatment in a hospital. At best, the patient is fully restored, with some greater sensitivity—which may persist—to cold in the affected areas. At worst, all or part of a foot, for example, may be lost.

The escape of body heat occurs insidiously, with growing lassitude and reduced energy combustion. It is not always discovered by the person affected, but rather by his companions. An essential measure is to continually check the condition of each member in a skiing group if the external conditions deteriorate. A generous intake of food rich in carbohydrate, with sufficient fluids, and good general fitness are the best insurance against risks of this kind.

Staying at high altitude

If you are a keen skier, you will probably one day want to practice your art in the high mountains, where suitable snow is guaranteed at least in the winter season. This may lead you to engage in hard physical exercise at higher altitudes than those to which you are accustomed. The air pressure falls as you go higher, and the proportion of oxygen in the surrounding atmosphere also diminishes. You must breathe in air at a greater rate than would be necessary to perform the same tasks at lower levels. Your reaction to the high altitude will be seen in breathlessness and fatigue after exertions that would otherwise cause you no problem at all.

For many people, altitude problems start at moderate heights, around 2,000 meters (6,500 feet) above sea level, although most of us begin to feel discomfort at 3,000−3,500 m (9,800−11,500 ft). Winter sports enthusiasts, particularly in North America and the Alps, often stay between 1,800 and 2,400 m (5,900 and 7,900 ft), while the surrounding peaks soar to over 4,000 m (13,000 ft). Here, the "thin" air becomes very noticeable and you find that going uphill is especially laborious. There may be other effects: slight headaches, a sensation of dizziness, and a poor appetite. Your food does not taste good, even if you are hungry when you sit down to eat. Difficulties with sleep may arise, with an inability to fall asleep, or with heavy sleeping that does not remove the general feeling of lassitude throughout the body.

Normally, these symptoms tend to disappear after a few days at high altitude, but the drop in efficiency remains. It is important to take things gently if you are spending a holiday of a week or so by touring on skis at high altitude. Allow generous rest days, especially at the beginning. If you stay for a rather longer period at high altitude, your body starts to become acclimatized: most importantly, the number of red corpuscles in the blood increases so that its oxygen-carrying potential is improved. The working capacity of the lungs will also increase so that more air is passed through them with each breath.

As skiing is the most probable reason for your staying at high altitude, you can reckon on a general improvement in your fitness—your sojourn, in fact, amounts to a period of training. For complete acclimatization at altitudes of, say, 2,000−3,000 m (6,500−9,800 ft), you must count on staying for three to four weeks with regular physical exercise. If you spend a shorter time at these altitudes, it would be reasonable to expect a more moderately paced holiday, with less strenuous skiing than you may have anticipated. Naturally, people differ in regard to how easily they adjust to the reduced oxygen supply. It is noteworthy that children are often more sensitive to changes produced by high altitude than adults are. People who suffer from heart ailments or have had such problems in the past should be particularly careful.

Ultraviolet radiation

Also associated with skiing at high altitude are the problems caused by intense sunlight. The dazzling snow, which reflects virtually all the light that falls on it, and the relatively clear, pure mountain air, contribute to the strain placed on the unprotected skin and eyes. The intense sunlight will probably give you a beautiful tan, but this is produced by a change in the skin which, if too rapid, can be very troublesome. It is important to protect your skin with a suitable cream, which should have a high capacity for filtering out most of the ultraviolet rays in sunlight.

Protect your eyes with dark sunglasses, preferably of a type that is shaped to prevent light entering from the sides. Even if the weather is not completely clear, ultraviolet rays can penetrate the cloud cover—especially at high altitudes—and may cause burns on the retina of the eye. This painful condition is known as snow blindness, since the affected person cannot see. Very dark glasses, and staying in a cool dark room, will relieve the pain and lead to recovery within a few days.

The great temperature changes and the cold winds of the mountains tend to dry out the body's mucous membranes. The lips, in particular, need to be protected with a special salve. At high altitudes, where sun and winds are strong, lip sores are a common problem and they easily become infected. If you work much with your bare hands in the snow—for example, when preparing food, using equipment for mountaineering, or repairing your gear—the skin of your fingertips will become brittle and crack. A good preventive measure is to rub your hands with a silicon ointment or another suitable skin cream.

Health hazards

Finally, you should realize that substances such as alcohol, tobacco, and certain medicines affect your efficiency and reduce your fitness. Alcohol "tricks" the body so that even small amounts open the fine blood vessels at the surface and increase the rate of heat loss. This can be fatal in a cold environment where the body should be conserving the heat it produces, not overtaxing its resources by losing heat quickly. The central nervous system is also affected by alcohol, which is a narcotic and diminishes the powers of judgement and rational thought. The breakdown of alcohol, which takes place mainly in the liver, decreases the body's capacity to store carbohydrates, and your reserves of this important fuel are consequently reduced as well, lowering your efficiency and making you tired more quickly.

Tobacco acts upon the body partly through the nicotine it contains, and partly through carbon monoxide in the smoke inhaled. Nicotine affects the central nervous system, the blood pressure, and the pulse. A smoker has a pulse-rate increase which is often ten to fifteen beats per minute faster than that of a non-smoker performing the same work. Carbon monoxide blocks the haemoglobin in the red corpuscles of the blood. The corpuscles are less able to take oxygen from the inhaled air as the monoxide replaces it and attaches more firmly to the haemoglobin than does the oxygen.

Some medicines also have a negative effect on your efficiency and imply risks where physical activity is concerned. If you are regularly taking medicine of any kind, you should consult your doctor about the exercise you engage in. Generally, however, physical exercise of the right kind in judicious amounts will have a positive effect, and may even speed up rehabilitation and recovery after illness. Always be careful about infections and do not resume training before an infection has cleared up. A slight cold or an irritation of the throat or mucous membranes is a sign that should tell you to take things gently for a few days. Sports injuries such as sprains, dislocations, cramps, pulled muscles, and so on, are also indications that you ought to slow down and become completely well before you resume your regular exercising or venture out on a skiing tour. Good general health is the best basis for cross-country skiing.

Equipment **2**

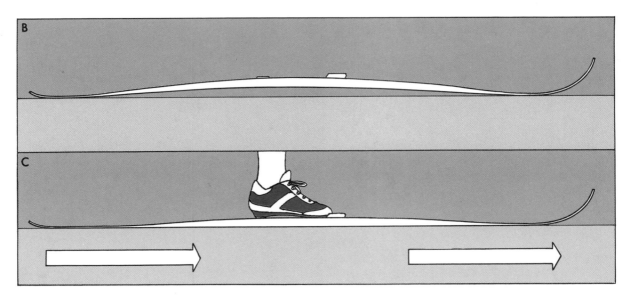

The 1960s were a crucial and an experimental decade in ski manufacture. Knowledge of new materials and construction methods increased, led by the Central European makers of downhill skiing equipment. Tests also took place with better running surfaces for cross-country skis. Such advances, together with over-production and much automation, created a considerable challenge to the traditional Scandinavian market in wooden skis. Synthetic ski materials achieved a complete breakthrough at the 1974 World Championships at Falun in Sweden, and have wholly prevailed since then. Skis entirely of laminated wood are still cheaper and are manufactured in large quantities around the world. But all the development has been in the man-made field with fiberglass, epoxy, and polyethylene plastics. These new materials have given us lighter and stronger skis with improved gliding characteristics.

Today there is an appreciable excess of cross-country ski production everywhere, due to optimistic assumptions about the size of the world market. Although interest in Nordic skiing has grown greatly in the past decade—especially in Central Europe and North America, once dominated by the Alpine viewpoint—the succession of winters with too little snow, and the establishment of too many firms in the trade, have resulted in large unsold stocks of skis. Advertisers try to promote cross-country ski equipment by the same means as in the Alpine sector, with more models and changes of fashion each season.

A The geometry of a ski is characterized by *(1)* the bottom camber and *(2)* the side camber which facilitates turning. Other parts are: *(3)* shovel, *(4)* tip, *(5)* shovel height, *(6)* tail. Competition skis have parallel sides or are boat-shaped with tapering front and back ends. These are only for well-prepared ski trails.
B An unweighted ski should be supported on the ground by only a small part of the front *(1)* and back *(2)* running surfaces.
C When the skier stands with equal weight on both skis, they should glide on the front and back running surfaces. The camber should support much of the weight without reaching down to the ground.
D If the skier stands on only one ski, its whole running surface including the mid-section will be in contact with the snow. The load is distributed over the entire ski but there is greater friction against the snow and the glide is worse than in the previous example.
E When the skier kicks off, the force exerted against the snow can be up to three times the body weight, providing forward thrust along the trail.

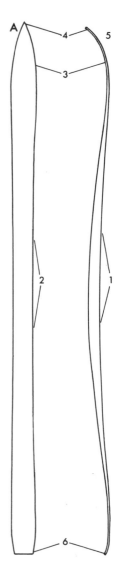

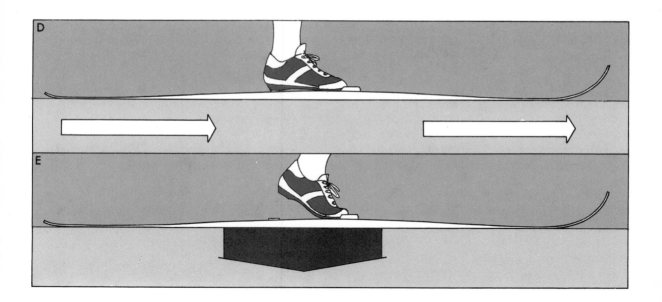

The shape of the ski

A long ski naturally gives you a larger supporting surface than a short one, but it is harder to maneuver on difficult terrain. Similarly, a broad ski offers more support than a narrow one, but it makes movement more laborious when traversing a slope, or when you must use the ski edges on a hard surface such as the icy snow of spring. To choose the right length of ski—which is rarely over 220 cm (7 ft) today—the simplest method for an adult is to stand with the hands raised above the head. The tip of the ski should then reach about to the wrist or to the palm of the cupped hand. When selecting the width of ski, one should study the different types of ski and the areas for which they are intended, as will be discussed later in this chapter.

Camber

Another important factor is the side camber, or waisting, of the ski. Most skis are widest at the shoulder, just behind the raised shovel at the front. They taper back to the narrowest point—about where the foot of the skier is placed—and then widen toward the heel, although remaining narrower here than at the shoulder. This shape gives the skier several advantages. The ski is more stable on rough trails and when moving straight ahead, as the frictional forces acting upon the heel of the ski always try to push it back on course if it deviates. If the skier sets the ski on its inner edge and puts weight on it, the friction is greater upon the shovel than upon the heel, so that the ski turns, sideslipping a little and following a curved path. By contrast, modern "extreme" forms of cross-country skis, with straight parallel sides, are primarily designed for competitive skiing or advanced training, and are meant to be used only on mechanically prepared trails.

The bottom camber, or arch, of the ski is among the key features in determining the performance characteristics. Camber gives a ski its elasticity and helps to distribute the weight of the skier over as large a part of the running surface as possible. However, the actual amount of bottom camber is less significant than the inherent stiffness of the ski—the force needed to flatten out the camber. If the skis have the right camber in relation to the weight and technique of the skier, the camber is not fully flattened when the skier places an equal weight on each ski. The movement will then be mainly a glide on the front and back sections of the skis. If the skier shifts more weight onto one ski and pushes forward, for example in executing a gliding step, the camber will be fully depressed, and the area under the foot makes firm contact with the snow. In general, the pressure under the ski varies through the different phases of a movement. A ski with too much stiffness—having a hard "flex"—can never be pressed down completely and continues to slip back, with little purchase on the snow. If a ski has too soft a flex, it will grip properly but will not glide well, and the wax under the center of the ski is worn out more quickly so that slippage results.

There are various ways of picking the correct camber for skis. The simplest is to place the skis with their bases facing each other. You should be able to hold them together with only a tiny gap between their centers, and then to press them completely together by using both hands. This is explained by the relationship of hand strength to body weight, and of body weight to correct camber. Another method is to place the skis on a very flat and hard surface, such as a floor or table. Stand upon the skis and get someone to slide a piece of paper underneath them. This should barely be possible, just in front of or behind the foot, when your weight is evenly distributed. If you shift more weight to one ski, the paper cannot be removed. Today, many sports dealers have instruments for measuring the flex of skis, while some manufacturers label their products—especially competition skis—according to the degree of flex and the suitable weight range. Otherwise, people choose the amount of flex in relation to the length of ski desired.

It is worth remembering that flex does not depend only on the skier's weight. Good technique with a powerful kick and gliding action demands a harder-flexed ski. Skis for mountain touring should be chosen with regard to the extra load of a pack weighing 15–20 kg (33–44 lb). Most skiers with no special requirements should choose skis with soft flex, in order to avoid problems with slippage which can tire even a relatively well-trained individual and turn a ski tour into a less than successful experience.

The elasticity and reverse camber, or bending line, of a ski are also significant for its performance. When a skier puts his weight on a ski and flattens the camber, the ski bends along its whole length if the load is big enough. The ski should bend along a smoothly rounded line so as not to spoil the glide, and the line should have no irregularities. If the flex is too soft, most of the load will be applied just below the foot, resulting in a sluggish sensation and a poor glide, although the grip will be excellent under most snow conditions and it will be easy to turn. Conversely, if the ski has too hard a flex, the shovel and the heel must carry too much of the weight, and the skier stands over the central section as if on a bridge that never touches the surface, making the movement bumpy and difficult to maneuver, as well as preventing the wax under the center from gripping the snow.

Judging your skis

If you do a lot of skiing with a backpack of any weight, this should be taken into account when choosing your equipment. It may be best to use a longer pair, or skis with normal length but harder flex. Boys and girls, and women of light build, must take care that their relatively short skis are not too hard-flexed and thus inclined to slip. A light but proficient skier manages a better kick and glide if it is possible to grip the snow by pressing down on the central section of the ski.

When you have selected a pair of skis with the right camber and flex, check that the two skis are really identical. Put them together, base to base, and look along them. If the skis have equal flex, the edges of their bases should lie flush when squeezed together. When this is done, the original contact points at the ends of the skis should not travel more than 2–5 cm (1–2 in): otherwise, the front and rear sections of the skis will not grip properly. Both skis, of course, must be perfectly straight and plane, or they will not glide well. A twisted ski or a concave running surface does not allow easy or enjoyable skiing.

It is possible to make skis with a soft flex but with greater stiffness at the center. This is especially relevant to competition skis for long-distance events, an area where top-level sports-

A The paper test is a simple way of judging whether the ski's flex is hard enough. *(1)* The person who will use the skis must stand with equal weight on both skis. If the flex is sufficiently hard, a piece of stiff paper can be slid back and forth under each foot. *(2)* If the body weight is shifted onto one ski, the paper is held fast. This test is adequate for experienced skiers. A softer ski than what the paper test would approve is preferable for untrained or passive skiers.

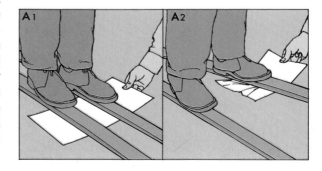

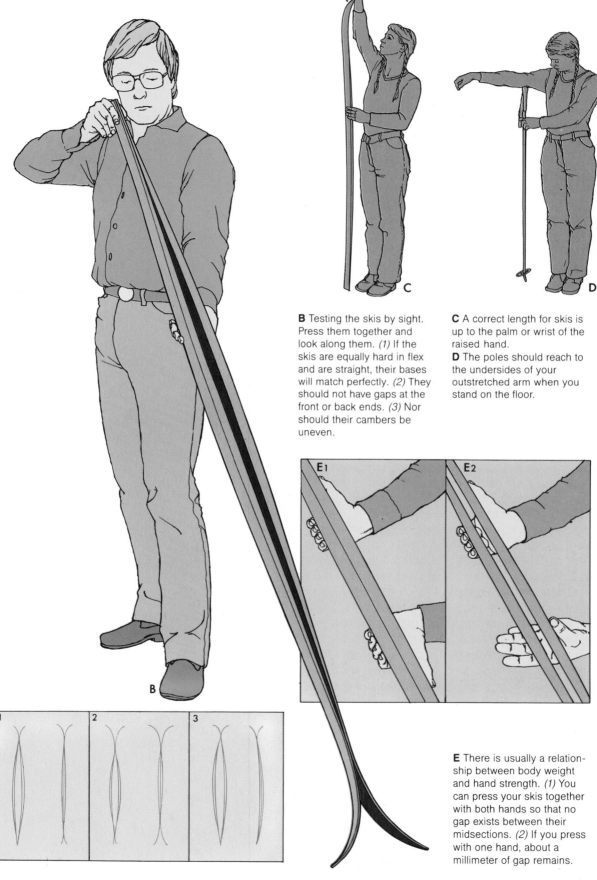

B Testing the skis by sight. Press them together and look along them. *(1)* If the skis are equally hard in flex and are straight, their bases will match perfectly. *(2)* They should not have gaps at the front or back ends. *(3)* Nor should their cambers be uneven.

C A correct length for skis is up to the palm or wrist of the raised hand.

D The poles should reach to the undersides of your outstretched arm when you stand on the floor.

E There is usually a relationship between body weight and hand strength. *(1)* You can press your skis together with both hands so that no gap exists between their midsections. *(2)* If you press with one hand, about a millimeter of gap remains.

men are continually experimenting to produce the best equipment for various skiing conditions. Skis for an icy trail, with snow temperatures just above or around the freezing point, do need a stiff central section: the skier uses the front and rear for maximum glide, and the center—prepared with klister—for good grip. Skis are also manufactured with a soft front and a harder rear section, in an effort to create particular skiing qualities.

The design of the shovels is important to the way in which skis "bite" on different snow surfaces. Skis that are specifically made for use on prepared trails usually have a tapering spear-shaped tip. Such a narrow pointed shovel has minimal contact against the edges of the ski trail and does not produce unnecessary friction when negotiating bends in the trail. This type of front end does not need to be especially long or sharply upturned. Touring skis, on the other hand, are required to perform well on soft snow and untracked terrain. On these skis, the shovel is both longer and more sharply upturned, while the front is markedly broader than the rest of the ski.

The bases

Ancient skis have been found with ridges along their running surfaces, or bases, as well as with broad concave grooves. Only at the end of the last century did the narrow tracking grooves, used on all modern skis, become universal. These grooves are intended to help the skis stay on course, although they are considered less significant today than the waisted central section and the heel design in determining the ski's tracking characteristics and its stability when moving straight ahead. Most cross-country touring skis still have tracking grooves, and racing skis—even if meant for use on mechanically prepared trails—sometimes have several grooves in their rear halves.

The ski base is the area which has undergone the greatest development in the past decade. While man-made materials are now predominant, especially in competition, wooden bases are by no means obsolete. On very cold surfaces and new snow, a birch-based ski is excellent for both glide and grip. Hickory and certain types of pine give an outstanding surface for wet and moist snow. All wooden bases, however, must be properly sealed and prepared, to preserve the natural qualities of the wood and to keep out the moisture.

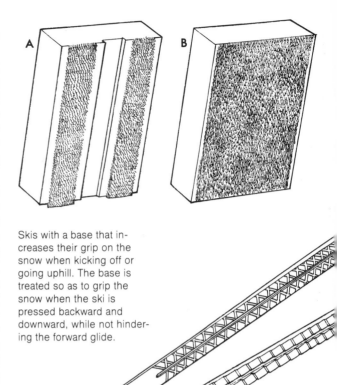

Skis with a base that increases their grip on the snow when kicking off or going uphill. The base is treated so as to grip the snow when the ski is pressed backward and downward, while not hindering the forward glide.

A Mohair strips let into the ski base. They can be either of real mohair or of some velvety material whose nap hairs are directed backward and rise up when the ski is pressed backward.
B A mohair rectangle covers the entire breadth of the ski.

C A negative base pattern is cut into the running surface.
D A positive base pattern is raised above the running surface.
E The herringbone pattern was among the first positive ones to be used. Its development here by Rossignol is called a wave pattern and varies in density, as do most base patterns, with the greatest density beneath the foot where the grip must be maximum.

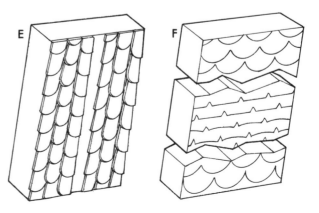

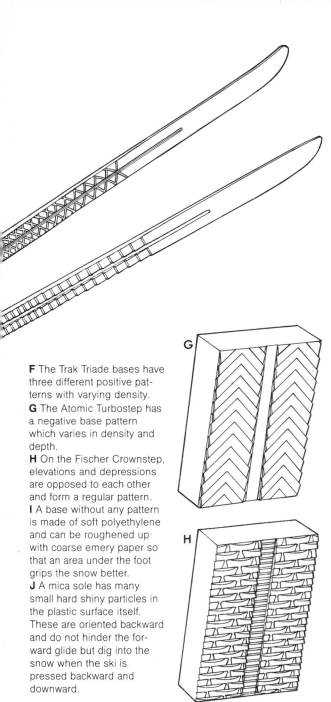

F The Trak Triade bases have three different positive patterns with varying density.
G The Atomic Turbostep has a negative base pattern which varies in density and depth.
H On the Fischer Crownstep, elevations and depressions are opposed to each other and form a regular pattern.
I A base without any pattern is made of soft polyethylene and can be roughened up with coarse emery paper so that an area under the foot grips the snow better.
J A mica sole has many small hard shiny particles in the plastic surface itself. These are oriented backward and do not hinder the forward glide but dig into the snow when the ski is pressed backward and downward.

Skis with synthetic running surfaces are a result of experience in downhill skiing, particularly in Central Europe. Some polyethylene plastics, with names such as Fastex and Kofix, were known to offer a very good glide under most snow conditions. The problem was to produce an acceptable degree of grip as well, notably for extended ski touring and hard snow. The traditional cross-country wax did not work properly on plastic, and other solutions were tried. The normal Alpine downhill covering, if mixed with a coarser medium to create a rough or "shaggy" coating, enabled the ski wax to stick better. A second method was to cover the front and rear sections with plastic of a different kind than that on the central section. A hard plastic covering was found to give a good glide and high durability, but a poorer surface for the wax. Soft plastic needed more frequent repair, yet provided a superb base for the various waxes.

For certain conditions when the snow temperature is around freezing, a ski requiring no wax to obtain perfect glide and grip has long been dreamed of. The early Scandinavians used animal pelts on their ski bases: elk hide, sealskin, and other kinds with short stiff hairs. Ski mountaineers still employ this technique when their "climbing skins" are glued onto, or stretched over, the ski bases. In a similar method, mohair strips about 1 cm (0.4 in) wide are let into the central section of the base on each side of the tracking groove. The strips need not be more than 30–45 cm (12–18 in) long if the skis have the right amount of flex. The wear on these man-made hairs will depend on how hard the surface is, but they can easily be replaced.

Mohair gives a good grip on most surfaces, even hard and icy ones—but it affects the glide, especially in severe cold. On a hard-surfaced slope where you have to ascend obliquely, your ankles must be turned outward so that the mohaired ski bases lie against the snow, for otherwise you will be skiing only on the edges and will get a poor grip. However, in the early spring when hard frozen snow remains on the heights, between the wet snow of the valleys and perhaps some new cold snow on the peaks, this type of base is very practicable. The American cross-country skier Bill Koch won an Olympic silver medal in the 30-km run at Innsbruck in 1976 on snow that was around freezing, with skis having mohair patches to give a good grip in conditions for which it was extremely difficult to find the right wax.

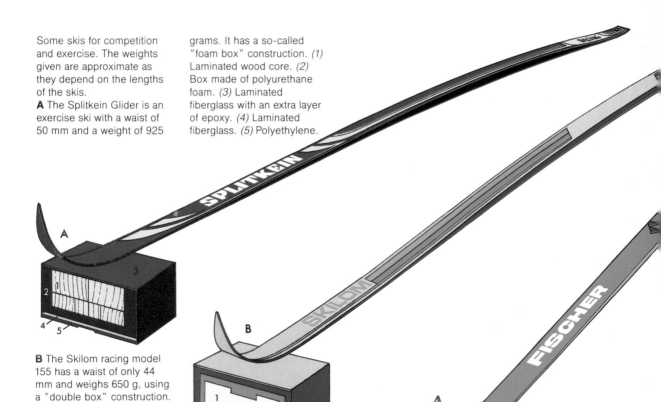

Some skis for competition and exercise. The weights given are approximate as they depend on the lengths of the skis.

A The Splitkein Glider is an exercise ski with a waist of 50 mm and a weight of 925 grams. It has a so-called "foam box" construction. *(1)* Laminated wood core. *(2)* Box made of polyurethane foam. *(3)* Laminated fiberglass with an extra layer of epoxy. *(4)* Laminated fiberglass. *(5)* Polyethylene.

B The Skilom racing model 155 has a waist of only 44 mm and weighs 650 g, using a "double box" construction. *(1)* Acrylic foam. *(2)* Epoxy/polyurethane. *(3)* Laminated fiberglass. *(4)* Polyethylene.

Another way to solve the problem of obtaining good grip without waxing is to cut a pattern of indentations into the ski bases. These patterns may resemble steps, fish scales, semicircles, and so on. They all grip the snow when pressed down and back along the line of skiing. A scored, uneven base naturally affects the forward glide to some extent, but this has little importance when skiing on a tour or for exercise, and waxing will help forward glide. The grip remains good in most conditions, although a whistling sound can be heard when you ski downhill—particularly on a rather hard surface—and it may be thought disturbing. A further answer to the glide–grip question is the base made of mica, a material whose structure allows the underside to feel smooth when rubbed in one direction, but rough in the opposite direction.

Regardless of the type of ski or the form of base, a correctly waxed and prepared ski gives the best glide and grip in most conditions. A mythology has grown up about the value of waxing, probably due to experience with special skiing conditions, such as temperatures around freezing and the variations in snow caused by changes in weather or altitude. Waxing a pair of skis correctly for normal conditions is not difficult.

The edges

A new method of reinforcing the edges of the ski bases was developed by Alpine skiers in Central Europe during the 1930s. It had been noticed that hard edges permitted easier steering and made wooden skis more durable on hard surfaces such as coarse frozen snow. These edges were created by screwing on segments of metal strips—using steel, brass, and eventually light metals—but they made the skis heavier and clumsier, and sometimes less elastic. For cross-country runs and ski touring, harder types of wood glued onto the bases were preferred, at first over the whole base area, and then in narrow strips along the edges. The woods employed were beech, hickory, and subsequently lignostone. The classic Nordic mountain ski, however, was fitted with screw-on steel edges for better performance on icy slopes. Alpine-ski technology has recently produced touring skis with one-piece edges of bonded aluminum, usually giving a good grip but not greatly influencing the weight or elasticity of the ski.

The plastic coating on the bases of modern cross-country skis normally provides a hard enough edge. Its main function is to protect the skis from excessive wear on the hard edges of

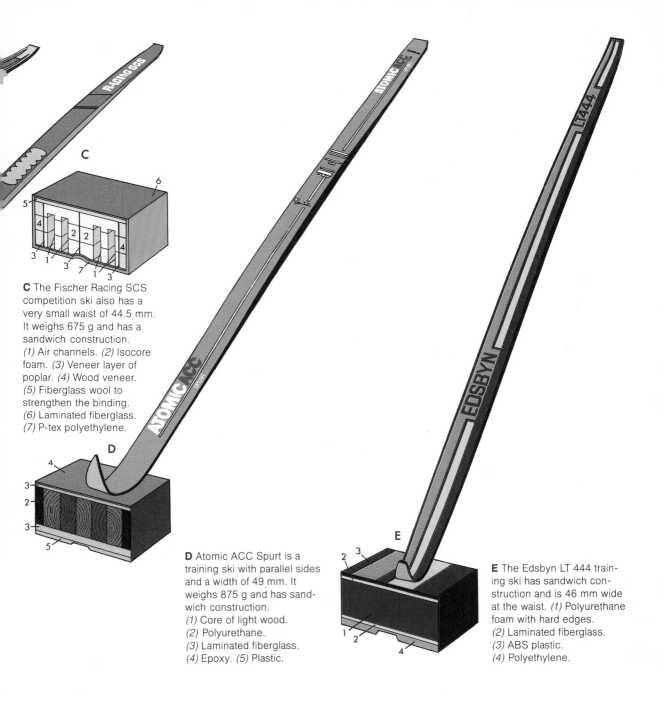

C The Fischer Racing SCS competition ski also has a very small waist of 44.5 mm. It weighs 675 g and has a sandwich construction.
(1) Air channels. *(2)* Isocore foam. *(3)* Veneer layer of poplar. *(4)* Wood veneer. *(5)* Fiberglass wool to strengthen the binding. *(6)* Laminated fiberglass. *(7)* P-tex polyethylene.

D Atomic ACC Spurt is a training ski with parallel sides and a width of 49 mm. It weighs 875 g and has sandwich construction.
(1) Core of light wood.
(2) Polyurethane.
(3) Laminated fiberglass.
(4) Epoxy. *(5)* Plastic.

E The Edsbyn LT 444 training ski has sandwich construction and is 46 mm wide at the waist. *(1)* Polyurethane foam with hard edges. *(2)* Laminated fiberglass. *(3)* ABS plastic. *(4)* Polyethylene.

the trails. Some competition skis also have this coating extended from the base and up the sides for further protection and to reduce the friction between the ski and the side of the trail. Orienteering skis are a special type with a steel or aluminum edge on the inside only, for a distance of 50–80 cm (20–32 in) in the central section of the ski. These skis are often used for travelling along plowed-up forest roads or firebreaks, where the skier can employ a skating technique to maintain speed on the hard, rutted surface instead of a more conventional diagonal stride.

Types of modern skis

Skis today are made almost exclusively for specialized purposes. It is therefore very important that you have a clear idea of what kind of skiing you intend to do mainly. Only then will you benefit by studying the various types of skis available.

Racing skis
Cross-country skiing at the level of competition or advanced exercise demands a narrow, light,

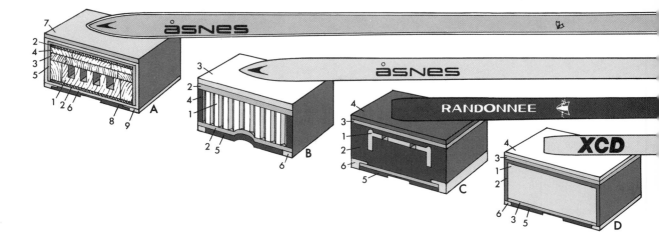

strong ski. As it is used solely on prepared trails, tracking characteristics are not the main priority. The ski should have a well-balanced flex, with an elasticity matched to the skier's weight and technique as well as to the prevailing conditions. Such skis are often constructed to minimize friction against the sides of the trail. Thus, they have narrow upturned tips and the plastic base coating extends up the sides. A single ski, if 210 cm (83 in) long, weighs 650 grams (23 ounces), with a width of only 45 mm (1.77 in) beneath the skier's foot. Racing skis require good technique and excellent balance in the skier if they are to be fully effective.

Training skis

This type of ski is somewhat broader and more stoutly constructed. It is made primarily for the skier who likes to exercise a little on prepared trails but also goes touring occasionally in nearby areas where the forest tracks are not always in the best condition. These skis have a slightly more pronounced waist than the pure competition type, making them better suited to untracked terrain or poor trails. They are about 50 mm (2 in) wide at the waist, and weigh a bit more than racing skis.

Touring skis

For the skier who is mainly interested in tours of home territory, but who also wants to make short mountain trips, there are skis either with or without reinforced edges of hardwood, plastic, or metal. These skis have a rather more marked waist than the two previous types, with a width of about 54 mm (2.1 in) at the center. Normal measurements at the shoulder, waist, and tail would be 63, 54, and 58 mm (2.5, 2.1, and 2.3 in)

to provide good stability and ease of turning.

Mountain skis

Although longer ski tours in early spring can be made on relatively light and narrow skis, even in mountainous terrain, most people would choose a broader and sturdier type for this purpose. Supporting capacity in soft snow depends on both the length and the width of a ski. As a skier in the mountains usually carries the extra weight of a backpack of 10–20 kg (22–44 lb), this too must be taken into account. A very skilled skier can certainly manage on the narrower and lighter type, but anyone uncertain about this should choose a broader, more generously built mountain ski. While its weight entails a further burden, this is offset by the increased stability. These skis are normally metal-edged and are slightly over 60 mm (2.4 in) wide beneath the foot. A long, flexible, and comparatively high shovel gives excellent buoyancy, particularly in deep soft snow and on uneven surfaces such as the hard, drifted snow of treeless mountainsides.

Forest skis

Other specialized ski types are manufactured for distinctive purposes, usually in limited quantities. The so-called forest or hunting skis are traditionally preferred by many people for upland work. They are produced in lengths up to 260–280 cm (102–110 in), with or without metal or hardwood edges, and the width under the foot is at least 65 mm (2.6 in).

Recently, several very short (150 cm, or 59 in) models have come onto the market for use in deep trackless snow. These have very wide waists, up to 105 mm (4 in), and are often called "gliding snowshoes".

Torsionbox T54

Honeyedge 62

ROSSIGNOL

KARHU

SUNDINS

trapper

FISCHER

TOUR EXTREME

bushwhacker   trak nowax

A Torsion-box construction of a Åsnes T54 touring ski, with a waist of 54 mm and weighing 1,050 g. *(1)* Wooden core with air channels. *(2)* Unidirectional glass fibers along the whole ski. *(3)* Laminated wood under the foot for the binding attachment. *(4)* Laminated hardwood. *(5)* Laminated fiberglass. *(6)* Box of laminated fiberglass. *(7)* ABS plastic. *(8)* Polyethylene. *(9)* Steel edge.

B A relatively new way to lessen the weight of mountain skis without decreasing their strength is to use a core of aluminum foil in a "honeycomb" form, as in this Åsnes Honeyedge 62 with a waist of 62 mm and weighing 1,125 g.
(1) Honeycomb core.
(2) Fiberglass matting. *(3)* Polyurethane. *(4)* ABS plastic. *(5)* Polyethylene. *(6)* Steel edge along the whole ski.

C Rossignol's Randonnée, with a waist of 54 mm and a weight of 650 g, is used extensively for untracked touring. The steel edges and marked side camber make it a good Telemark ski.
(1) Aluminum profile.
(2) Polyurethane.
(3) Polymerized fiberglass.
(4) ABS plastic.
(5) Polyethylene.
(6) Steel edge.

D Karhu XCD is also a Telemark ski. Somewhat narrower in the waist than the last model, at 52 mm, it has the same side camber and weighs 595 g. *(1)* Karpor core of solid plastic. *(2)* Plastic shell. *(3)* Fiberglass. *(4)* Polyurethane. *(5)* Polyethylene. *(6)* Steel edge.

E The Bushwhacker from Trak is called a "gliding snowshoe". It is only 150 cm long and has an incurved waist of 81 mm. Such short, wide skis have become very popular for those who want to wander outside trails in forest country with deep snow.

F Sundin's Trapper is a very wide (105 mm) and short (180 cm) forest ski, good for deep snow and difficult terrain. The base has transverse grooves for better grip.

G Fischer's Tour Extreme is a haute-route ski. It resembles a shortened downhill ski and weighs 1,350 g, with a waist of 69 mm. The shovel has a hole for attachment of a rope for carrying up or down a cliff. The steel edge is sawtoothed to give a good grip on ice.

H The Tegsnäs is a forest ski, made by hand with a traditional design, in lengths up to 285 cm. It is 75 cm wide and works well on loose snow.

Telemark skis

Another special-purpose ski developed in recent years is the Telemark, a touring ski designed for turning. It needs to be relatively soft, with a smooth flex curve, and the edges should grip particularly well on hard surfaces. Good torsional rigidity and damping characteristics are also essential. Suitable proportions have proved to be 62 mm (2.5 in) just behind the shovel, 52 mm (2.05 in) at the waist, and 57 mm (2.2 in) at the heel. The central section must be at least 8–10 mm (0.3–0.4 in) narrower than the widest part of the ski.

Haute-route skis

Another special type is the Alpine ski for high mountain touring. This is generally constructed on the same lines as the ordinary downhill ski, but it has softer flex, slightly greater width, and a harder, better-wearing surface for gliding. It is often fitted with a rope hole or a snap hook in the shovel so that it can be hoisted up steep glacier slopes, and it may have a groove for easier attachment of skins when climbing. These skis are usually available in lengths of 170–190 cm (67–75 in) and have Alpine touring bindings (see below).

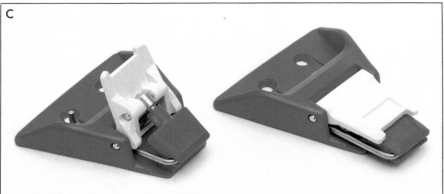

Bindings are nowadays standardized so that there is full compatibility between the ski, boot, and binding. This arrangement is called the Nordic Norm. The angles of the boot sole's inner and outer edges are specified, as are the number and mutual locations of pins on the binding. The allowed sole widths are 71, 75, and 79 mm, but in some cases 83 mm exists as well.

A The cable binding is made in ever smaller quantities and is commonly replaced by the clamp binding.
B A clamp binding is simple and functional. It suits both light racing and training boots as well as stronger touring boots. The strongest type has a connection for toestraps, and a ring to attach a ski-brake strap which prevents loss of the ski if you fall on steep terrain.

C The racing binding requires a special extended sole on the ski boot. This is because the modern machine-made cross-country ski track, cut out of the snow cover, has sharp and hard-frozen edges whose friction against the binding must be minimized. The racing binding comes mainly in two models: Racing Norm (also called Norm 50) and Norm 38. These differ in

regard to the shape of the sole front. Norm 50 has two or three pins (with the same separation as Nordic Norm) which fit into the sole's underside, and a distinctive shape of the part which clamps the sole front. Norm 38 has a pad on the front part which is fastened directly to the binding. Both types are identical on the left and right sides. The racing binding is very light and is

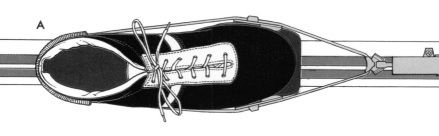

Ski bindings

The earliest skiers attached skis to their feet by means of leather straps which passed through a vertical or horizontal hole in the ski. Some prehistoric skis also had raised strips to give the foot more lateral stability. For a long time, leather thongs were normally used to make a toe binding, or toe and heel bindings—a simple artifice, quick and easy to take off and put on, for example when hunting. Adjustment and repair were equally simple. The rigid heel binding is thought to have been devised in the mid-nineteenth century and, according to some authorities, was pioneered by Sondre Norheim of Telemark. Tightly twisted birch branches, fixed to the broad toestrap, formed a binding that made it possible to turn the whole ski with the foot, while leaving the heel free to move vertically.

It was particularly in Norway that the ski binding began to evolve. At the end of the last century, Huitveldt created a type of binding with a fixed toe iron and a strap which buckled around the heel. Subsequently a metal lever was added to tighten the binding when the foot was in place. This type, patented by Høyer-Ellefsen in 1904,

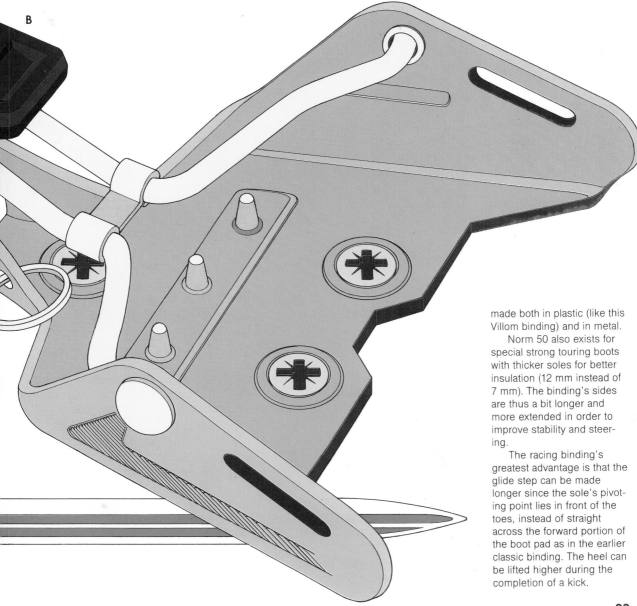

B

made both in plastic (like this Villom binding) and in metal.

Norm 50 also exists for special strong touring boots with thicker soles for better insulation (12 mm instead of 7 mm). The binding's sides are thus a bit longer and more extended in order to improve stability and steering.

The racing binding's greatest advantage is that the glide step can be made longer since the sole's pivoting point lies in front of the toes, instead of straight across the forward portion of the boot pad as in the earlier classic binding. The heel can be lifted higher during the completion of a kick.

dominated the market until 1930. The fixed metal toepiece was, however, replaced in the 1920s by Marius Eriksen's adjustable type, with a horizontal metal plate screwed onto the top of the ski after passing through the horizontal toestrap hole.

Cable or wire bindings

The development of Alpine skiing in the 1920s and 1930s demanded a binding that would allow free upward movement for the heels when skiing up a slope and, for the downhill runs, would enable the skier to apply his whole foot to the ski to achieve better steering. Cable bindings were one solution but, as with all compromises, they have several weaknesses. They are relatively heavy and clumsy, and tend to wear out the wire sheathed in the cable so that it breaks at inconvenient times. The low hooks for cable attachment must be screwed down hard to avoid bending the wire at too sharp an angle. The ski boot should have a well-defined groove in the heel to prevent the cable from slipping down at the back. In addition, the cable must be properly secured to the base of the binding—preferably screwed down, glued, and stitched as well—for otherwise there is a risk of the heels coming loose if the skier falls forward. The cable should have some form of spring loading to reduce the chance of its snapping under tension. The lever in front of the toepiece should be attached to the ski by at least three screws, and ideally it should close by dropping back toward the skier. The length can be varied by changing the size of the cable or by tightening the binding by means of the lever. Today, the best cable bindings are made of light metal and have toepieces standardized according to the Nordic Norm (see below).

Clamp or pin bindings

A quite different principle was offered by the Bergensdahl binding in 1913, and later developed into the "Y" and Rottefella bindings. A spring-loaded metal clamp grips the front of the ski boot, which is also held in place by the side pieces of the toe housing, together with two to four metal pins that fit into corresponding holes in the front part of the sole. Such a binding allows the heel to be lifted freely and gives the foot a greater degree of mobility than in earlier types. This is especially important in competition and makes a longer gliding step possible. Various models of these bindings exist, and the most robust versions are eminently suited to the stur-

dier kind of ski boot as well as to long ski tours. Manufacturers of bindings have agreed on a "Nordic Norm" which standardizes measurements and angles of bindings and boots, so that they all fit each other regardless of the maker. The bindings come in three sizes: narrow at 71 mm (2.8 in), normal at 75 mm (2.9 in), and broad at 79 mm (3.1 in).

Racing bindings

With the breakthrough of laminated plastic skis in 1974, as already noted, racing bindings to be used with flanged boots became generally available to the public. The advantages were a smaller and lighter unit of binding and ski boot, a mininum of protruding parts which caused friction against the sides of the ski trail, and a lengthening of the glide step by placing the boot–ski attachment point in front of the toes. The drawback has been that only certain makes of bindings and boots can be combined.

This type of binding, known as the "Racing Norm", comes in widths of 38 mm (1.5 in) and 50 mm (2 in). The flange of the boot, a forward extension of the sole, is gripped by a small clamp or secured by a metal rod that passes vertically through it. Unlike clamp bindings, this type is symmetrically mounted so that the left and right skis are interchangeable. Today, top skiers and cross-country practitioners who compete or exercise regularly are using this type of binding almost exclusively. Development is continuing, and integrated binding systems of boot–toe fastening–heelplate have been introduced. The Salomon SR Racing and Adidas Racing Norm are of this type. The most important feature of all these bindings is that the ski boot drops into the right position in relation to the center line of the ski, with no lateral play between the binding and the boot.

One problem of ski touring and cross-country work is that, in some circumstances, snow sticks between the boot sole and the upper surface of the ski, deterring performance. A solution is to fix plastic plates with little friction under the foot, so that the snow slides off instead of building up. Heelplates with a flexible rubber "popper" can also prevent snow from sticking.

Heel supports to aid turning

With attachment points in front of the toes and with very light, supple ski boots, great lateral pressures are exerted, especially when changing direction and controlling movements at

A reliable touring boot for cross-country skiing in hilly or other difficult terrain. Competition boots are much lighter and lower in the ankle. *(1)* Padding. *(2)* Tongue to keep the boot's upper part watertight. *(3)* Hook. *(4)* Eyelet. *(5)* Leather upper, to which the tongue is sewn. *(6)* Sole. *(7)* Heel. *(8)* Groove for cable binding, with a low fastening point.

speed. Assistance is provided by various types of heel support which fix that part of the boot on the upper surface of the ski when the heel or the whole foot is under load. These supports may consist of a serrated plate, or one or more raised strips that grip the heel of the boot. The Salomon binding has a "control" ridge which fits a groove in the front part of the boot sole. Other manufacturers, such as Adidas, have a plate with a high, longitudinal, triangular profile that fits in a corresponding track in the heel of the ski boot.

These devices help the skier to control and turn the ski when his foot is pressed fully down on it, and to relieve the pressure particularly on the front part of the binding. A similar method is to fix a kind of spur, or "heel locator", on the back of the heel. This projecting spur fits into a fork which is screwed in place just behind the heel. The arrangement does not hinder the vertical movement of the foot, but it effectively blocks all lateral movements when the whole foot is loaded and pressed onto the ski. The result is an efficient transfer of the required steering force to the ski.

On the stronger clamp-type bindings, and on bindings with metal toepieces, it may be convenient to use a toestrap as an extra aid. There are often special notches for toestraps on the sides of the bindings. If the clamp or cable breaks, a toestrap enables the skier to reach a place where spare parts or repairs are available.

Ski brakes

A simple and very practical aid, notably when skiing in steep terrain and deep soft snow, is the ski brake. This single leather or nylon strap, secured to the binding and passing around the skier's ankle, is an excellent safeguard against lost skis. In the event of a fall, the foot sometimes comes loose from the binding and the ski slides away if there is no strap to retain it. Losing a ski can be fatal in untracked country far from habitation.

Alpine ski bindings

For touring in high mountain country it is advisable to use specially designed skis and bindings. These bindings function in exactly the same way as the ordinary Alpine type when skiing downhill, with a mechanism that releases the foot sideways when the twisting forces acting on the leg are too great, and with an upward-releasing arrangement at the heel. For climbing, the skis are provided with mohair skins and the bindings are undone to allow the heel to be lifted freely. The whole binding is usually mounted on some form of plate, set immediately in front of the stout ski boot. In extremely difficult conditions—steep slopes and hard frozen snow—the binding can be augmented with special blades (called "Harscheisen" in German) which cut down into the snow on each side of the boot to improve grip and lateral stability.

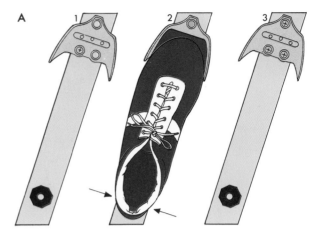

A Mounting the bindings. If the ski is not marked at its midpoint, this must be found by balancing it. Mark a line 10 mm (0.4 in) behind this and place the binding so that the two outer pins are just on top of it. *(1)* Use an awl to mark the place for one of the two rear screw-holes. Bore the hole and thread it with a tap, especially if the ski has sandwich construction. Screw on the binding through the hole. *(2)* Attach the boot to the binding and position the heel in the middle of the ski. *(3)* Hold the binding in this position and remove the boot. Mark, bore, and thread the other holes, then tighten the other screws. Dip the screws in a multicomponent adhesive in order to seal the holes and fasten the screws properly. If the ski is very narrow, be careful that both rear holes are equally far from the ski's outer edge.

Fixing ski bindings

Correct placement of bindings is essential if the best use is to be made of the qualities built into the ski. It is easy to fix a ski binding if you study the manufacturer's instructions carefully and have the right tools. If you are at all doubtful about it, a professional should do the job. Usually, there is a mark on the ski to indicate where the toe of the boot must be placed. Many bindings are also accompanied by a template to show precisely where to drill the necessary holes. Later, when you fasten the ski boot into the binding and raise it with your ankle relaxed, the ski will tilt forward slightly, so that the tip remains correctly positioned in the track: the ski should be somewhat front-heavy in this way, to give good characteristics of gliding and tracking.

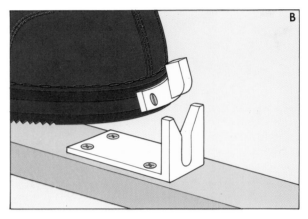

B For downhill runs on cross-country skis, and especially when making Telemark turns, a heel support is very useful. Shown here is a so-called heel locator. Its spur is screwed to the heel and fits into a fork which is screwed onto the ski.

Boots for cross-country and ski touring

A boot for cross-country skiing should be light, supple, and able to withstand the pressures and strains exerted continually at the points where it is attached to the bindings. It should also keep the wearer's foot warm and dry while he is skiing. Modern cross-country ski boots look very much like lightweight training shoes and allow the wearer complete freedom of movement of foot or ankle. In the past, leather was mostly used—such as strong supple kangaroo hide—but nylon uppers and composition soles are common today. Competition boots are cut low, beneath the ankle, and should be bought large enough for the toes not to rub at the front. Check that there is no creasing over the toes when the boot and the sole are bent sharply with upward movements of the heel.

On many cross-country boots, the laces are protected by an extra tongue held in place with Velcro strips to stop the entry of snow and dampness. As the cross-country skier is normally active during the whole of a journey, he produces enough heat to keep his feet warm, so that one pair of socks is sufficient. For exercising and for the easier tours, somewhat stouter boots are available. These should also be cut low, beneath the ankle, and preferably made of leather with a softer material around the top to fit more snugly. The sole is quite thin in order to fit a clamp binding or Racing Norm 50. There must be ample room for the toes, and perhaps for an extra pair of thin woolen socks. The sole is vulcanized onto the leather upper and is made of some type of rubber. Check that there are holes drilled into the underside to take the pins of the clamp binding.

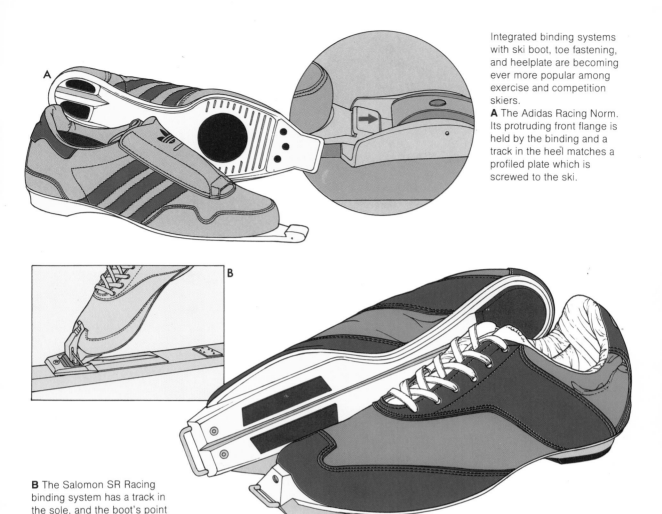

Integrated binding systems with ski boot, toe fastening, and heelplate are becoming ever more popular among exercise and competition skiers.

A The Adidas Racing Norm. Its protruding front flange is held by the binding and a track in the heel matches a profiled plate which is screwed to the ski.

B The Salomon SR Racing binding system has a track in the sole, and the boot's point of attachment to the binding is a metal ring.

For slightly longer day tours, and for ski touring in mountain country, a stouter boot is required to provide better insulation against the cold and to offer more support at the skier's ankles. This type of boot must reach above the ankle and have a thicker sole. The tongue is usually provided with tough padding, and sometimes the boot is double-laced to give a closer fit. Opinions are divided as to whether a ski boot should be lined: several layers will generally improve insulation, but such a boot needs more time to dry out if it becomes wet. The main function of a ski boot, of course, is to attach the skier firmly to the ski by means of the binding and to support the foot adequately, while warmth and insulation can then be obtained with long socks and snow gaiters of suitable shape. Leather is an excellent material which, if correctly

treated, keeps moisture out and at the same time allows the foot to breathe.

In early spring and when the temperature rises toward or above the freezing point, the snow becomes very damp and watery, so that it may be virtually impossible to keep the feet dry in leather boots. Boots made entirely of rubber, with cloth linings, are well suited to these conditions. Another good solution is a type of boot made of cellular rubber with leather ankle-shafts of various heights. This boot is completely watertight underneath and, due to its leather shaft and a leather lining, still gives the foot ventilation.

For high Alpine touring an ordinary downhill ski boot, not too high and not angled too sharply forward, can be worn. The skier should be able to stand upright with his legs straight when at rest, but should have the required support for downhill skiing. The sole must be shaped to function safely with the release binding. The market today offers special high mountain boots that are light, comfortable, and practical. In appearance, they suggest a cross between a mountaineering boot and an Alpine ski boot.

Any good boot for mountain touring must have a generous sole to insulate the foot from the cold surface, and preferably one with a non-slip profile. Whatever type of ski boot is chosen, it should give the skier adequate room, especially in the toe, supporting the foot while allowing complete freedom of movement. Inside, the sole should provide the instep support, and the boot should not have too much lateral play. It must be rigid enough along its length to ensure that the skier does not put his heel on the side of the ski when turning his foot. Check the fit of the boot in the binding, and choose a sole whose surface is not too slippery.

A Ski poles are manufactured for purposes that range from racing, touring, and exercise to long tours in high mountain terrain. *(1)* Handgrip made of insulating material, with an anatomical shape and, ideally, slanted somewhat forward in relation to the shaft. *(2)* Wrist strap made of good quality leather or woven nylon. It should be well attached and not too narrow. *(3)* Buckle of metal or plastic to adjust the strap length.

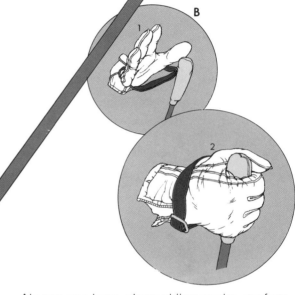

(4) The shaft determines the pole's quality and price. It may be of Tonkin bamboo, metal (usually aluminum alloy), or carbon fiber. *(5)* The basket is normally made of vinyl plastic, which is soft and flexible even at low tem-

peratures. Its size depends on the area of use, and varies between 8 and 15 cm (3.2 and 6 in) in diameter. It should be properly attached but also easy to change if broken. *(6)* The tip, or spike, should be made of hard metal and inclined somewhat forward. This helps the skier to maintain purchase in the snow even when the arm swings the pole back.

Always use long, clean skiing socks, preferably of good quality wool. Take one or more pairs, depending on the type of skiing and the external conditions. In very severe cold, you can employ the old trick of pulling a large woolen stocking over the boot before it is locked into the binding. Various kinds of special boot coverings are available today, particularly for the thinner competition models, and work quite well. Gaiters are another indispensable aid on long tours or in deep snow. These are made of natural or nylon cloth and may be long or short, with or without zip fasteners. They protect the vulnerable ankles from cold, and simultaneously stop snow or damp from getting into the boots. Good snow gaiters also cover the laces and reach up to just below the knee, keeping the skier's feet appreciably warmer and drier for long periods. There are also smaller, shorter gaiters that can be used with the light cross-country competition and exercising ski boots.

B The skier gets a good support around the wrist by *(1)* putting the hand through the strap loop from below and *(2)* taking hold of the handgrip. The buckle should be on the outer side of the hand. Make sure that the strap is not too thin—otherwise it may cut into your skin when you ski without gloves—and that it does not twist in your palm.

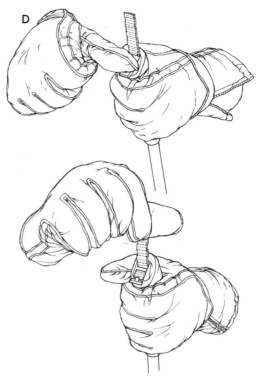

D

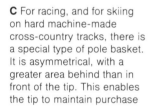

C

C For racing, and for skiing on hard machine-made cross-country tracks, there is a special type of pole basket. It is asymmetrical, with a greater area behind than in front of the tip. This enables the tip to maintain purchase in the snow even when the pole is pointing far forward, as on an uphill slope with hard snow. Note that the tip itself is angled forward. Such poles are very light, with shafts of carbon fiber. They have small light baskets of soft plastic, up to 8–9 cm (3.2–3.6 in) wide, usually oval or triangular in shape, and often mounted obliquely on the shaft.

D Some handgrips have a strap that can be adjusted without a buckle. The strap goes through the handgrip's upper part and is secured by a toothed groove or similar device. It can be made longer or shorter as required, and it locks in the desired position when tension is put on it.

Ski poles

The origin and development of the ski pole are uncertain. People probably skied at first without using their arms, and later aided their progress with the spear or bow normally carried for winter hunting. The use of two poles of equal length became general only at the end of the last century. Ski poles with spearpoints protected by a sheath of reindeer or elk antler, or with a digging tool or scoop at the end, were customary among Lapp herders until modern times.

The cheapest material in use for pole shafts, bamboo or straight-grown "Tonkin", is light and elastic, and relatively strong. A tendency to dry out and split can be prevented by winding a bandage tape around the shaft at intervals. Various qualities of fiberglass and metal are also employed for shafts: fiberglass is light, strong, and very elastic, while steel poles are much sturdier, although heavier and stiffer. Aluminum alloys have proved suitable for making shafts, with a tube that usually tapers downward to give a balanced pole that is light, strong, and elastic, its price being determined by the quality of the alloy. Carbon fiber is a new material, light and strong but expensive, used especially for competition equipment.

Skiers need a degree of elasticity in their poles to help push themselves forward. A strong, competitive skier who uses the modern poling technique will choose a harder pole, whereas the less-trained recreational and touring skier manages better with a rather softer, more flexible pole.

Ski-pole grips are made of injection-molded plastic or of insulating materials such as cork covered with real or imitation leather. Grips must be insulated and should allow a relaxed but steady grip on the pole. The grip is generally thicker at the top—the platform—to enable the pole to remain in the fold between the thumb and index finger when the hand is opened and the arm is extended backward in diagonal action. The strap, which supports the skier's wrist and prevents loss of the pole, should be of high-quality leather or nylon. Plastic straps are less suitable as they tend to become stiff at low temperatures. The strap should be adjustable, since a skier partly regulates his body temperature by wearing gloves or mittens of varying thicknesses, which must be accommodated. Biotechnical research has shown that slanting the grip and the upper part of the pole slightly forward facilitates the wrist action and allows the skier to carry the pole tips forward more easily.

The baskets, or snow rings, prevent the pole from sinking too far into the snow. Most baskets are circular and they vary from 8 to 15 cm (3 to 6 in) in diameter. The smaller models are best suited to well-prepared ski trails where the poles grip well, while the bigger types are better for skiing in deep snow and trackless terrain. The baskets should be light, strong, and made of a flexible material—usually plastic—and should be easy to change if broken. Asymmetrical baskets, normally used for exercise training and racing,

Children learn to ski more easily than adults do. They are not as afraid of falling and their ability to grasp basic techniques intuitively is greater.

A Ski poles suitable for children should not have sharp tips since these could cause injuries. The poles serve at first only as an aid to balance and are used very little to help the child move forward. The tips should be blunt and made of some rubbery material or soft plastic.
B A good binding for the child gives great freedom of movement at the heel but also lateral stability in turning the foot. The toestrap makes it possible to use different kinds of boots depending on the season, from ski boots to rubber ones.

are designed to give the tips maximum grip in hard surfaces and on ascents, even when the poles have a pronounced forward slant.

The tip, or the whole of the pole below the basket, is often angled forward. This gives the skier more purchase from the very beginning of the pole movement, and the tip continues to hold even at the end of the arm movement. The tip should be sharp and preferably of hard metal. It may need sharpening after the poles have been used on a hard snow surface or when the cover is thin.

The size of the basket is the most important consideration for high mountain touring. Poles should not be too short here, as you will often have to ski in soft snow and on steep slopes. An excellent additional aid in the mountains is a kind of extension that enables two poles to be screwed together to form a snow probe, 2.5–3 m (8–10 ft) long, if their baskets and grips are easily removable. The probe can be used when looking for suitable snowdrifts to bivouac in, or when an avalanche accident occurs. For ski touring in upland and high Alpine areas, this is a key item of safety equipment.

Ski equipment for children

Even very small children like to play in the snow and to do it with skis on their feet. Since their powers of concentration are not great, the equipment must be easy to take off and put on again as their interest changes. Skis that are too short will make balancing difficult, and a preferable length is 10–15 cm (4–6 in) greater than the height of the child. The skis must not be too narrow, but should have the appropriate waisted "Telemark" shape for better stability and tracking.

A sufficiently soft wooden ski, correctly primed with tar, is excellent to begin with. It is most important that the flex is not too hard, because the child's light weight and un-developed technique will otherwise render the ski difficult to manage and prone to slipping. The combination of wood and fiberglass—preferably with a non-wax running surface (see pages 32-33)—will give even a short ski acceptable soft-ness, grip, and glide. The fiberglass base cover-ing makes the edges quite hard enough. Waxing

is vital except on non-wax skis, and the child should be helped with this by an adult. It is best to choose a rather softer wax than the temperature and snow conditions suggest. A child's skis must grip properly when going uphill and moving directly ahead.

The binding should be easy to use: ideally, a child can put on and take off his own skis. The "Gresshoppa", a Norwegian binding with a toestrap and a movable footplate having a heel housing and anklestrap, is excellent and can be employed with various types of ski boots, from felt or leather to rubber in the spring when the snow is wet. A child's version of the clamp bind-ing is good but requires special boots with cor-rectly shaped front parts. Cable bindings are needlessly expensive and often difficult to adapt and fit. In fact, the development of a better bind-ing for children is still awaited from the ski manufacturers.

Ski boots for children should be warm and roomy enough for at least two pairs of woolen socks. Children are more readily affected by cold than adults, and lack the adult's capacity for con-sciously maintaining body temperature by physical activity. At regular intervals, a child should be allowed to remove the skis and play in the snow without them, so as to get warmed up and not become bored with skiing.

Children can manage quite well without poles and are, indeed, quicker to learn correct patterns of movement if permitted to ski without poles. Ski poles for children may be of Tonkin bamboo or fiberglass and should reach up to their armpits. The grip must be easy to hold and, at first, a strap is undesirable. Plastic straps that become stiff are particularly unsuitable for young children and difficult for them to handle. When straps do prove necessary, these should be adjustable for different thicknesses of gloves. The pole tips must not be too sharp-pointed for children, who use poles only as an aid to balance.

Waxing cross-country and touring skis

Why is it that a ski will glide better on one occasion than another? What causes the skis sometimes to grip well and next to feel hopelessly heavy? When a ski moves forward, small drops of water are produced by the friction between the base of the ski and the top layer of snow crystals. This thin film of water is what enables the ski to glide. If the snow is extremely cold, insufficient heat is created by friction, and the skis seem to drag. When the snow is damp, or even wet, at temperatures above freezing, the water retards the ski and it does not glide well. In this case, the ski bases must be treated with a coating of grease which makes them smoother and more water-repellent.

If the weighting of a ski is increased, when the skier kicks or is checking his forward movement, the top layer of snow crystals does not melt uniformly. The sharp edges and star-shaped projections of the crystals press into the base of the ski. The base may have a correct degree of hardness, or it may be treated with the right kind of wax, so that the snow crystals penetrate into it and provide an adequate grip. If the wax is too hard or the ski is not treated at all, the snow will not grip on it and it will slip back. But if the wax is too soft, the snow crystals penetrate too deeply and stick there—the ski "ices up" and will not glide well in either direction. These complications would be easier to deal with if snow were a stable material having fixed properties. The real situation can be understood by studying the formation of snow crystals.

When the temperature falls below freezing, small drops of water are deposited on dust particles in the air, and snowflakes begin to form. Their shape and size depend on the amount of moisture in the air and on the temperature, but each snow crystal is hexagonal, with unique features, and it may consist of sharp ice needles or of more flat compact disks. While falling, the snowflakes are worn down and rounded by the wind. As soon as they reach the ground, a process of change starts. The snow settles slowly and the crystals are broken down into fine grains, which later build up into coarser grains, at a rate that increases with the temperature. After a few days, the beautiful crystals have usually disappeared and been replaced by coarse "corn" snow. This is sometimes melted in strong sunshine and freezes again into coarse, sharp ice crystals, forming the crusty snow known as

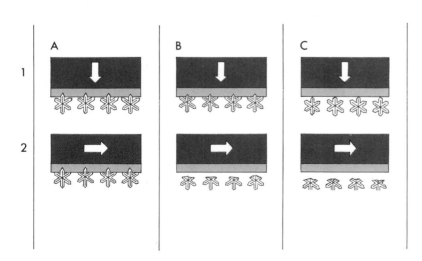

The choice of ski wax must be suited to the temperature and age of the snow. (1) In kick phase. (2) In glide phase.
A The wax is too soft or its layer is too thick. The snow crystals stick too deeply into the layer, giving excessive friction.
B Properly waxed. The wax and snow are equally hard, so that the ski has good grip and glides easily.
C The wax is too hard. Snow crystals do not dig into the layer, resulting in poor grip and glide.

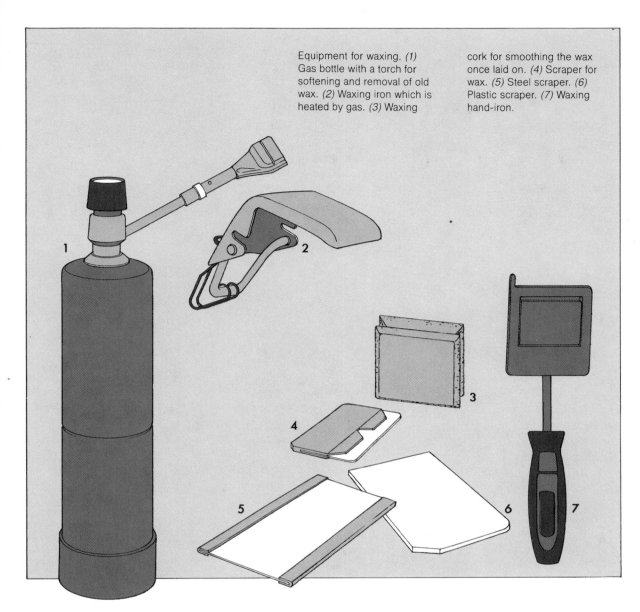

Equipment for waxing. *(1)* Gas bottle with a torch for softening and removal of old wax. *(2)* Waxing iron which is heated by gas. *(3)* Waxing cork for smoothing the wax once laid on. *(4)* Scraper for wax. *(5)* Steel scraper. *(6)* Plastic scraper. *(7)* Waxing hand-iron.

"skare"—or in the summer it becomes fine snow at high altitude on the glaciers and snowfields. The final building-up phase results in ice crystals, a few millimeters wide and hollow in the center, which are called cup crystals.

In order to choose the right type of wax for skis, we must be able to judge the age and nature of the snow surface. It is enough to distinguish between *newly fallen* snow, whose crystals have not yet changed perceptibly in form; *fine-grained* snow, which is more compacted and often accompanies new snow; and *coarse-grained* snow, consisting of large well-rounded grains. The appearance of the surface may vary greatly, as when skare is created by the freezing of damp "corn" snow into a continuous crust, and when

new snow or fine-grained snow produces slippery, glassy ski trails that are different from the surrounding snow cover.

We need further information to judge the skiing conditions of the day correctly and to choose a suitable wax. The water content of the snow is determined by temperature. Below freezing, the temperature in the upper layers of snow is about the same as the air temperature. Above and near the freezing point, this is not true, but you can judge the consistency of the snow by feeling it with your gloved hands. *Dry* snow falls apart and flies away in the wind, while rather *damp* snow holds together like a ball, and snow is termed *wet* if water drips from it or the surface becomes moist when you squeeze it.

Types of wax

To many people, it may seem that some kind of magic is involved in waxing cross-country and touring skis. This is by no means the case, and the basic principle is very simple. Low temperatures yield cold snow with sharp crystals that require a hard wax. Temperatures around freezing, or damp snow with coarser and more rounded crystals, demand a softer wax which prevents the ski from sticking in the wet and still provides a good purchase on the snow. Such

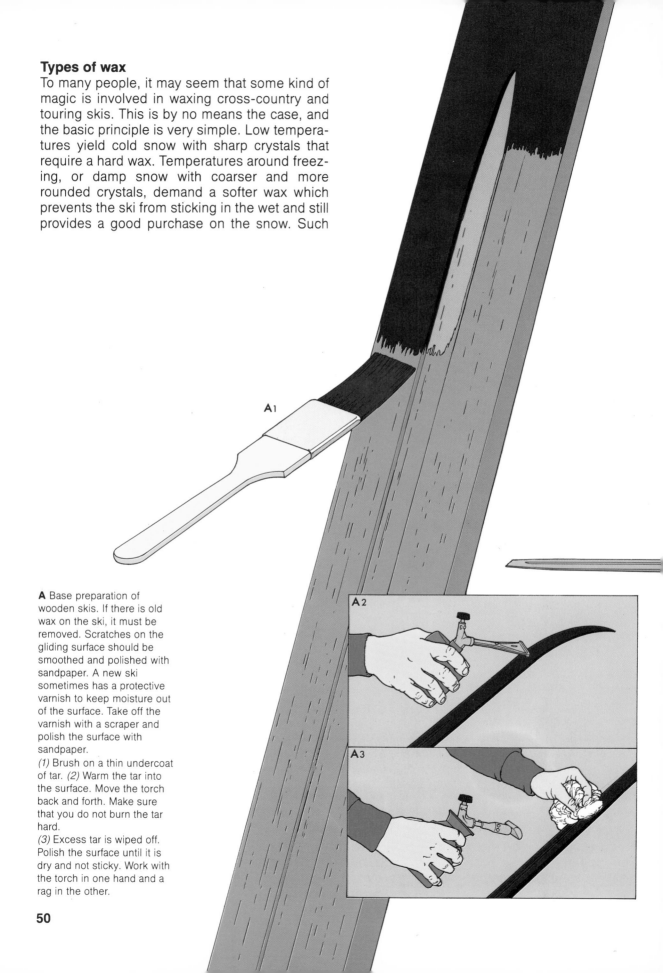

A₁

A Base preparation of wooden skis. If there is old wax on the ski, it must be removed. Scratches on the gliding surface should be smoothed and polished with sandpaper. A new ski sometimes has a protective varnish to keep moisture out of the surface. Take off the varnish with a scraper and polish the surface with sandpaper.
(1) Brush on a thin undercoat of tar. *(2)* Warm the tar into the surface. Move the torch back and forth. Make sure that you do not burn the tar hard.
(3) Excess tar is wiped off. Polish the surface until it is dry and not sticky. Work with the torch in one hand and a rag in the other.

A₂

A₃

waxes are generally known as glide or running waxes.

On modern synthetic skis with stiff camber, we can divide the base into three areas. The front and rear sections, which mainly support the skier's weight when he glides or stands on both skis, are waxed purely for maximum glide, and the waxes used are almost the same as for downhill skiing. The central section of the ski, extending 80–100 cm (32–40 in) forward from the back of the ski boot, is the part that is employed for the kick in the diagonal stride action, and it must be waxed to give a good grip when weighted and pressed down into the snow.

Wax manufacturers now largely use a common "international color code" to mark their various products. Warm colors, such as red and yellow, indicate soft waxes for wet snow; cool colors, like blue and green, indicate hard waxes for dry, cold snow. Essentially, we can distinguish between three types of wax: cold waxes, klister waxes, and klisters.

B Base preparation of skis with polyethylene bases. *(1)* Melt the paraffin wax with a waxing iron over the whole gliding surface. The ski should lie horizontally. *(2)* The paraffin is smoothed out with the warm waxing iron. Let the skis lie for at least half an hour so that the paraffin becomes cool and somewhat stiff.
(3) The paraffin is scraped away with a plastic scraper. Only a thin film should be left on the ski. Always move the scraper in the forward and backward directions. *(4)* Take away the paraffin from the tracking groove with a rounded plastic scraper. Then rub the gliding surface with a clean waxing cork.
C Waxing table. The colors are standardized according to the international norm.

(1) Yellow klister for wet snow. *(2)* Yellow klister wax for mushy snow. *(3)* Red wax for snow in transition to damp. *(4)* Red Special wax for falling snow in transition to damp. *(5)* Violet wax for snow in transition from damp to dry. *(6)* Blue extra wax for almost dry snow. *(7)* Blue wax for dry snow. *(8)* Green wax for powder snow. *(9)* Green Special wax for falling powder snow. *(10)* Polar is the hardest wax for dry snow. *(11)* Red klister for wet fine-grained snow is the softest of all klisters. *(12)* Silver klister for wet corn snow and for a surface varying from dry to wet. *(13)* Violet klister for coarse-grained snow, varying from icy to wet. *(14)* Blue klister for dry coarse-grained snow, skare, and ice. *(15)* Green klister for icy trails.

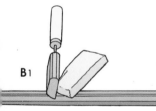

B1 B2

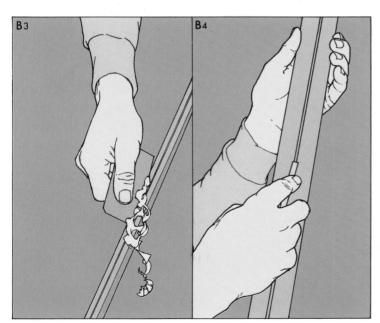

B3 B4

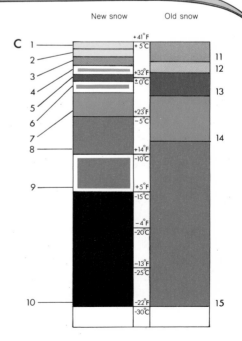

New snow   Old snow

C 1
2
3
4
5
6
7
8
9
10

+41°F
+5°C
+32°F
±0°C
+23°F
-5°C
+14°F
-10°C
+5°F
-15°C
-4°F
-20°C
-13°F
-25°C
-22°F
-30°C

11
12
13
14
15

Preparing new skis

New skis must be treated in a special way for best effect, and there is a difference between skis with wooden and with synthetic-coated bases. A wooden base has to be impregnated with tar, which protects it against penetration by moisture, makes it harder and more durable, and provides a better surface for glide waxes to adhere to. If this work is done carefully, it will keep the skis in good condition for a long time. However, if you ski much on hard icy surfaces, you may need to repeat the tar treatment several times during the season.

Skis with a hard synthetic coating of the epoxy type always require glide waxing in order to grip. It may be advantageous to treat the base with a base or "sealer" wax which is melted on and polished. This gives a better key surface for glide waxes to stick to, and durability will be considerably improved.

Skis with bases that are rough in texture, or sometimes of almost "hairy" polyethylene, need a preliminary treatment with some type of paraffin-based wax. The microscopically small hollows in the plastic must be filled with the paraffin, so that the surface feels smooth to the touch and the ski glides better. This surface treatment also helps the glide waxes to adhere better and protects the plastic coating from oxidization.

General hints on waxing

You should first get a small stock of waxes from the same manufacturer. Read the labels to learn the intended areas of use, and then go out to build up your own experience. Gradually increase your selection of waxes, and try some more difficult skiing conditions, such as those for klister and around the freezing point. You will soon find that waxing is easy and skiing on well-waxed skis is a delight.

Wax preferably at room temperature. The skis must be dry and clean, and tarred or otherwise pre-treated.

The colder the snow, the harder the wax should be, and the thinner the application. For long ski tours and hard icy trails, several layers of the same wax are generally required.

Several thin layers of wax, each well rubbed in and polished, are better than a single thick layer. However, thick layers of wax tend to give a better grip.

Klisters should be applied by means of a blowtorch. Always clean your skis after a tour on which you have used klister wax, since it makes

A1

the process easier for the next ski tour.

If you are uncertain which wax to use, choose the harder one first. You can always apply a softer wax over a harder one, but not the reverse.

You need to ski at least a few hundred meters before you can properly judge whether you have picked the right wax and applied it with the right thickness. Before placing the skis on the snow to test glide and grip, stand them outdoors to cool down.

Backslip

If you are still experiencing backslip in spite of all precautions, the reasons may be:

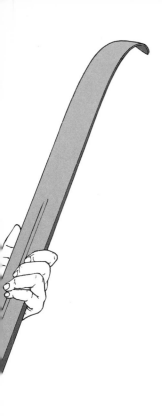

Waxing of skis is easiest at room temperature. See that the skis are dry and clean.
A Waxing with a hard wax for dry snow. *(1)* The wax is smoothed on with short precise strokes. *(2)* Spread the wax into an even layer with the cork. A waxing iron can also be used. It is best to put on several thin layers.

B Waxing with klister for wet snow. *(1)* Lay a string at each side of the tracking groove. *(2)* Even out the klister with a scraper or with your fingers.
C Klister can also be bought as a spray and evened out with a sponge which is provided with the container.

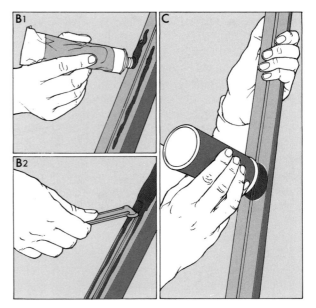

—Your skis are too stiff and you cannot press down the flex so that the snow crystals "bite" on the layer of wax.

—Your technique is poor. The kick is started too late or is not strong enough, or your skiing is unrhythmical.

—The wax is too hard and the snow crystals cannot penetrate into the surface. Try first with a thicker application of the same wax, then with a somewhat softer wax.

—The grip wax has been worn away. Apply a new coat. Check the tarring where appropriate, or prepare the skis with a suitable base wax for better wear.

Conclusion

Cross-country and ski-touring equipment is found in very many forms and in diverse qualities. It is most important for you to decide which type of skiing interests you particularly. Then you should choose all your equipment— skis, boots, ski bindings, and poles—so that they function well together as a unit in the preferred area of use. Within each discipline, from cross-country skiing for exercise and recreation to the extremes of ski mountaineering, it will be possible to make your selection on the grounds of economy and personal wishes and needs.

The manufacture of skis

The first skiers made their own skis, like other functional equipment. Wood was the natural material to use: for example, ash and beech in southern Scandinavia, or birch and pine in central and northern areas. Craftsmen developed great skill and artistry in decorating skis with beautiful ornamentation and engraved designs. A particularly prized material for skis came from conifer trees which were leaning over, yet trying to grow straight, so that the trunk was bent upward and the wood on the side nearest to the ground became dark and very hard. This part was excellent for skis used on thawing surfaces, as the snow did not stick to the skis.

The increased demand for skis made it feasible to establish small factories in the 1890s, but the old handcraft methods tended to continue. Laminated skis, the most important of all innovations in ski manufacture, were known at an early date and their extensive production began in the 1930s. The upturned "shovel" at the front of the ski could then be given its permanent moulded shape, in contrast to the older carved or steamed varieties. Another introduction was American hickory, a strong and durable wood: skis made entirely of it were almost impossible to wear out, and needed no waxing, although they became somewhat heavy and clumsy.

Manufacturers started during the 1920s and 1930s to reinforce the edges of skis with metal strips of diverse patterns. These may have been developed initially for Alpine skiers, but the classic Nordic mountain ski was also usually fitted with metal edges. At this time, ski equipment was still not nearly as specialized as in later years. Skiers used the same pair of skis for a long mountain tour, jumping, or racing downhill! The pure competition ski for cross-country events, however, did begin to take on its unique form, becoming both narrower and lighter.

It was chiefly in Norway and Finland that the originally utilitarian ski was developed into a piece of equipment for sport and recreation. The first documented ski contest was organized in Norway as early as 1843, and a farmer named Sondre Norheim—from the village of Morgedal in the district of Telemark—invented methods which are basic to much of modern skiing. The "Telemark turn" began with his technique of slowing down on a steep slope, and better performance was achieved by skis with a tapering, waisted "Telemark" shape. Norheim also made a binding from birch branches which enabled the skis to be turned with the feet as required, instead of only moving straight ahead.

A notable stimulus to interest in skiing was the journey made on skis by Fritjof Nansen across the inland ice of Greenland in 1888, as described in his book about it. Significant, too, was a ski race organized in 1884 by the Arctic explorer A. E. Nordenskjöld from Sweden, where a distance of 206 km (128 miles) at Jokkmokk in the north was covered in just 21 hours and 27 minutes by the winner, a Lapp named Pavva-Lars Tuorda. Such races became very popular, often being held between rival towns. Especially around the end of the nineteenth century, skiing was taken up by people who had never tried it or needed to ski in daily life. A fashionable sport was born and its "Nordic", aspects, long-distance skiing and ski jumping, began to develop.

Technique 3

The technique of cross-country skiing is not particularly difficult to learn. It is based on the same natural pattern of movement that you use when you walk, jog, or run. Our movements, of course, seem complex if we take into account all the muscles that are involved in the work, and the small adjustments that we have to make in different situations in order to keep our balance and at the same time move the body in the direction and in the manner which we decide. But it is no more necessary to analyze your movements in such detail when you begin to ski than it was when you first learned to crawl and jump.

The essential thing is to be fully aware of the movements, accustoming yourself and your body to a new situation where function and economy of movement should be the guide. As a beginner, you must concentrate on what you are doing so that you can sense what is, or is not, functioning well. In this way, you will gradually increase your technical skill and also learn continually to adapt your technique to external circumstances. Snow conditions, terrain, and equipment affect your technique and it is your strength, resilience, and suppleness that determine how quickly and elegantly you can move on skis.

Forward movement

When you have selected suitable equipment and made sure that your skis are properly waxed—it is especially important in the beginning that they grip well—you will find it easiest to start practicing on level ground with prepared ski trails. These will help you to steer your skis so that you need only concentrate on moving ahead. It may sometimes be useful to practice on a slight incline, so that you can really feel yourself pushing the skis forward. If a downhill slope makes the skis start to glide too fast, your movements become too quick and you do not achieve a rhythmical action.

Your first exercise with skis on your feet can be just to walk forward, taking steps no longer than you can manage without feeling the skis slip back. Be sure to practice lifting the tail of one ski while you stand still and try to keep your balance on the other for a few moments. Train both your legs in this way, without using your ski poles to balance. Remember that the skis should be kept parallel so that the tips do not splay outward and you start to tread on your own tails. In the beginning you will fall over a great deal, feeling stiff and awkward—this is quite normal. To fall over and

When you pole without glide steps (see pages 64–65), it is mostly the shoulder and stomach muscles that are used. The hands pass just below knee height as you shift from the pull phase (when the poles are used for pulling yourself forward) to the push phase (when you bear against the poles). At the end of the push phase, the poles are swung forward to begin a new plant and pull phase.

The force for driving forward as you kick off *(1)* comes mainly from the seat and leg muscles. The skier stands on the supporting leg (here, the right leg) and glides forward in the so-called glide phase. When the kickoff ends, the other leg swings forward and becomes the new supporting leg. During this leg's forward swing *(2)*, the pole plant for the pull phase begins *(3)*, to end in a push phase. When the pole plant ends, the pole swings forward *(4)* to begin a new plant. A certain forward driving force also results from the pole plant.

pick yourself up again is a natural part of the learning process which you must go through when teaching yourself new movements. Watch how toddlers learn to walk: it is a matter of not giving up but continuing to practice.

You are accustomed to making diagonal movements while walking or running. When one foot is placed down, the arm on your opposite side swings forward to harmonize with the backward push of the foot. The more vigorously the legs and feet work, the bigger the arm movements become. The whole process is fluent and rhythmical, characterized by alternations between rest and effort. Since the legs perform most of the work, and are usually better exercised than the arms, it is advisable to begin to practice without ski poles. Let your arms hang loosely by your sides, and feel yourself gliding carefully on the snow. To increase this gliding sensation, you could take off one ski and practice with the other, not forgetting to do so with each leg in turn. Strive for a smooth forward movement, rather than letting each glide last too long. If you close your eyes, you will get a better idea of how the ski slides over the snow, and every uneven part of the trail underfoot will be noted.

When you try to push forward a little more vigorously, you will notice that you must lean the upper body further forward. It is important that these movements should not be exaggerated at first and cause the skis to lose grip and slip backward. Practice gently and methodically. Only through long and purposeful practice will your movements become so instinctive that you can be considered a proficient skier. Your first attempts with ski poles should also be made gently, using the poles to help you move forward and not primarily to keep your balance. It is very easy to develop the bad habit of always supporting yourself on your poles, and this is why you should begin skiing without them in order to train your sense of balance on skis alone.

When you feel that the glide is beginning to work for you, and you can ski with fair speed, choose a trail with a moderate downhill slope—preferably one that subsequently flattens or slopes slightly upward, as this will help you to stop. Next, practice getting in and out of the trail on either side, by shifting first one ski and then the other. Glide gently forward on both skis and bend down to pick up objects from the ground. Make sure that you are standing on the whole of your foot and can easily move your ankles, knees, and hips. Practice also stretching yourself up and crouching down while the skis are gliding forward.

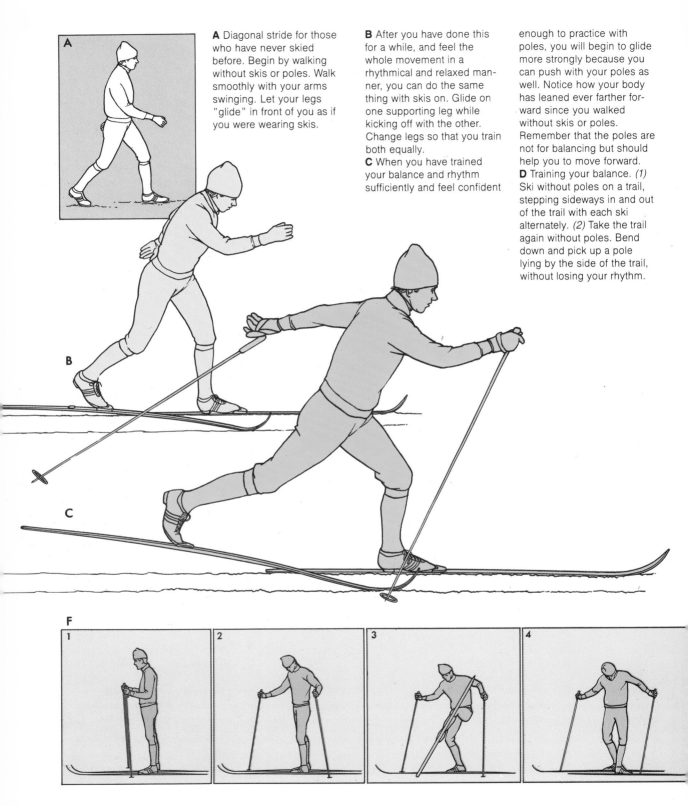

A Diagonal stride for those who have never skied before. Begin by walking without skis or poles. Walk smoothly with your arms swinging. Let your legs "glide" in front of you as if you were wearing skis.

B After you have done this for a while, and feel the whole movement in a rhythmical and relaxed manner, you can do the same thing with skis on. Glide on one supporting leg while kicking off with the other. Change legs so that you train both equally.

C When you have trained your balance and rhythm sufficiently and feel confident enough to practice with poles, you will begin to glide more strongly because you can push with your poles as well. Notice how your body has leaned ever farther forward since you walked without skis or poles. Remember that the poles are not for balancing but should help you to move forward.

D Training your balance. *(1)* Ski without poles on a trail, stepping sideways in and out of the trail with each ski alternately. *(2)* Take the trail again without poles. Bend down and pick up a pole lying by the side of the trail, without losing your rhythm.

F The kick turn is a good way of turning around as well as of training your balance. *(1)* Initial position. You want to turn in the opposite direction. *(2)* Plant your poles firmly in the snow as shown. *(3)* Lift up one foot so that the tail of your ski is clear of the snow surface. *(4)* Put down the ski with the tip in the opposite direction. *(5)* Now you must move your left pole to the right side of the right ski. Next, lift up the right ski and swing it around so that it lands parallel to the other ski. *(6)* You are now pointing in the desired direction.

58

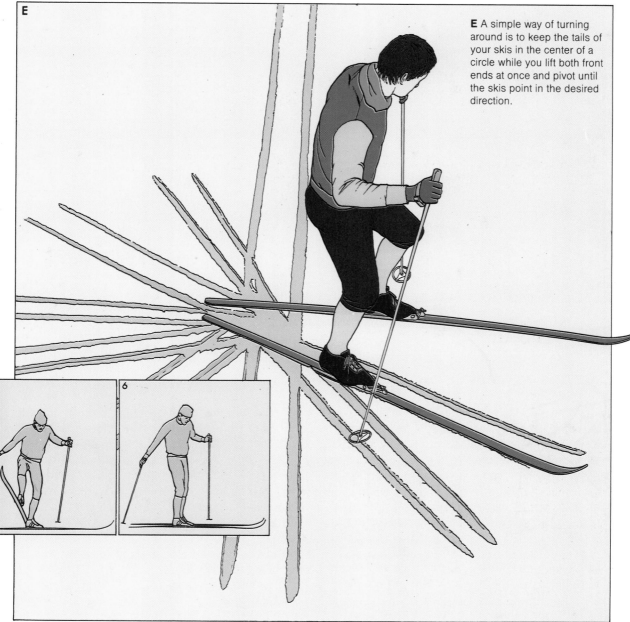

E A simple way of turning around is to keep the tails of your skis in the center of a circle while you lift both front ends at once and pivot until the skis point in the desired direction.

In the two-beat diagonal stride, try to make your kicks powerful and decisive, rather than staying in the glide phase too long. When you have finished extending the leg that kicks off, your weight has shifted to the other ski and you are gliding forward. The kickoff leg then swings up and back so that the ski's tail lifts from the snow. It is characteristic of the two-beat diagonal stride that both poles are in the air at that point. A pole is planted at an acute angle in the snow, about on the level of the gliding foot and with the hand well forward. At the same time, the kickoff leg begins its return forward. The pole effort consists firstly of a pull phase until the hand is about on a level with the thigh. Next, the effort is completed with a push phase so that the forward force becomes as effective as possible. The arm and pole finally swing back and up in a relaxed way, depending on how strongly the movement is carried out. By opening the hand and turning the palm a bit inward and upward, the pole can be directed more freely. Let the pole grip rest between the thumb and forefinger.

The two-beat diagonal

This is the most usual technique for skiing on level ground and up gentle inclines. You move forward by extending the muscles around the hips, knees, and ankles. Pole work should be helpful, but most of the effort comes from the leg muscles. As the most natural and relaxed way of skiing is with the legs relatively straight and the area of your hips rather high, any unnatural sitting posture should be avoided. The kick with the foot, beginning when the two feet are level with each other, should be directed as far back as possible. Depending on how strong a kick you have, your upper body must lean forward so that the movement ahead is dynamic and purposeful. If you ski with your body too upright, the force of your kick goes straight down into the snow: you will grip well, but your forward movement will be small. If instead you lean too far forward, the ski will slip and you soon become tired. When your purchase on the snow is poor, you will sometimes need to start your kick sooner than is normally required.

The more powerfully your legs work, the more vigorous your arm action will become in the same fluent pattern of movement. Do not use

poles that are too long, as these can make it harder to achieve rhythm in your skiing. All your poling should be parallel to the trail, close to your skis, and aimed at pushing you forward. A common fault of unpracticed skiers is to plant their poles out to the sides because of poor balance.

It is important that the back and its muscles are also involved in the work, but without exaggerating lateral movement. Anyone who has grown unaccustomed to skiing is prone to back fatigue, but a properly executed pole action and good weight transference can help to minimize the affliction. Although proficient skiers may be

seen to bob up and down as their center of gravity rises and falls, this motion should not be overdone.

With a well-executed kick, you sense the forward movement throughout your body. The muscles of your seat and the extensors in your knees and ankles should perform most of the work. Remember to keep your shoulders relatively low when the relaxed hands, arms, and poles swing forward after each completed effort. You should keep looking forward so that you are ready for the various situations and changes that may arise on the trail.

The muscles of the back and arms which are affected in the two-beat diagonal can be rested if you changed to the four-beat diagonal, by skipping two pole plants while swinging the poles forward easily, as shown below. The diagram above exhibits the pattern of the four-beat diagonal. Pole plants are represented by the circles, and gliding steps by the skis. The two-beat diagonal uses one pole plant per gliding step (glide-plant, glide-plant, and so on), whereas the four-beat diagonal uses two fewer pole plants for every four gliding steps (glide-plant, glide-plant, glide, glide, and so on).

The four-beat diagonal

For the infrequent skier it may be laborious to ski using both arms and legs constantly, as in the two-beat diagonal stride. Sometimes, too, the trail is such that the poles do not grip well. More or less unconsciously, you may then miss one or more pole plants without disturbing your rhythm. Primarily to spare the back muscles, but often also when skiing with a pack and needing to straighten the upper body occasionally, the four-beat diagonal is employed. After doing two glide steps with the corresponding pole action, the skier makes the following two kicks without using his poles, which swing gently forward in the meantime and are planted much further in front than usual. Then two gliding steps are executed in the normal way with pole planting, then two without, and so on. You will be able to sense which rhythm and tempo suit you best.

Pole action

Modern cross-country technique, well-prepared trails, and the development of skis with ever better running surfaces have made poling technique ever more significant in this branch of the sport. It is customary to distinguish between poling without a glide step and poling with one or more glide steps.

Poling without glide steps

When poling without kicking, both poles are planted at the same time and at a sharp angle to the snow. You must bend your trunk forward so that you can pull on both arms as early as possible. The legs should be fairly straight and the hips high when the movement is started. If your arms are slightly bent, you will usually be able to pull more strongly. Use the muscles of your shoulders and stomach, and continue to lean forward from the waist. Because of the angle of your body, your hands will pass directly below the knees on the way back. Continue the whole movement of your arms through the push phase until your palms are turned inward and upward. At this point, the upward movement of the body is begun and the poles swing forward, ready for the next step.

Poling is appropriate when you have a good glide and the trail may be sloping slightly downhill. Utilize the falling motion of the upper body to come up to and past the poles, and avoid gliding in a sitting position with the legs bent.

Poling without glide steps. (1) Completion of the last poling. The body rises up and the skier begins to swing the poles forward. (2) Initial position. The poles are planted at a somewhat acute angle in the snow. (3) The skier lowers his upper body forward and pulls with the poles. (4) The push phase begins as soon as the hands have passed the leg. The upper body is bent well for-

Poling with glide steps. (1) The skier finishes the last poling. (2) Initial position. The foot which kicks off (the left foot here) is somewhat in front of the supporting leg. (3) The left foot kicks off powerfully. Avoid bending the supporting leg too much while you glide. When you finish kicking off, the pole action is only beginning. At first, the poles make an acute angle with the snow. The kickoff leg is swung forward and the upper body is bent forward so that as much as possible of the body weight can be used in the pull phase. The hands pass

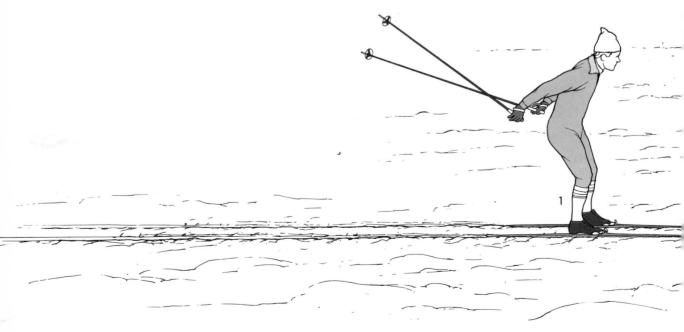

64

ward. The pole angle against the snow should now be as small as possible. *(5)* The push phase ends and the arms are stretched backward. The grip on the poles has relaxed and the hands

are turned inward. The upper body rises up and the skier completes the poling before taking up a new initial position.

Poling with glide steps

To increase the force of your forward thrust still further, it is usual to perform one or more kicks while both poles are carried forward, before starting the double poling action. The kick must be initiated early so that you can easily come up to and past the poles. Here, too, you should avoid gliding with the supporting leg bent: this is fatiguing and is not a good preparation for the following pole plant.

the leg just below the knee height. The arms are fully extended at the end of the push phase, while the poles are slackened and the hands are turned inward. Relax your arms as much as you can when returning to the initial position.

Skiing uphill

The simplest way of climbing a slope is probably to side-step, either straight up or across. Edge the skis slightly and then move one ski at a time. So long as your skis are parallel and at right angles to the fall line, you will not glide forward or backward. If necessary, you can support yourself with both poles simultaneously, one above you and the other below, so that you always have three points of support. Do not take too long a step. This method of climbing can be used even on very steep slopes, and on hard surfaces, providing that your skis have good, sharp edges.

Another method is the herringbone, named after the pattern which the skis make in the snow. The tips of the skis are splayed out—so wide apart that, by using your knees, you can press the inner edges of the skis into the snow. Steadying yourself with the poles can be a great help. Be careful not to get your skis and poles tangled. As the ski tips are so far apart, the poles must be planted a little further out to the sides, but not so far that you cannot manage to push on them. The steeper the slope, the more you must turn out the tips: the skis in fact form a reverse of the "snowplow" position. Strong skiers climb with the diagonal stride, almost bouncing from ski to

If an uphill slope is not too steep, you can "herring-bone" up it, as these children are doing. The ski tails should be near each other, with their tips opposed so that the skis form a V. The knees are pressed inward to place the skis on their inner edges. The diagram shows how you support yourself on your poles.

ski as they make their way up very steep slopes.

The two-beat diagonal uphill

If your skis are properly waxed and the trail is a good one, you can try using the two-beat diagonal stride even on ascents. For as long as possible, maintain the same steady rhythm that you had before starting uphill. If the slope becomes steeper, you will have to shorten your stride and push forward more vigorously with the leading foot. You must also lean forward from the waist and, above all, avoid any tendency to ski in a sitting position. When you begin your kick, the weight of your body must be carried well forward.

The poling action becomes shorter and the front pole is not planted as far forward as in the diagonal stride action on level ground. It should be planted roughly level with the heel of the front foot, and even further back if the hill is really steep. The rear pole keeps its grip on the snow until the front pole is secure. On steep hills you also have to push forward and upward to place the weight of your body over the supporting leg for a better grip and kick.

Do not try to jump uphill: rather you should practice on small inclines until you feel that you can ski uphill fluently and securely without having to change your diagonal-stride rhythm much.

If the uphill slope is steep, you may sidestep up it. With the skis straight across the fall line (which is the direction your skis would take if you lost them, right down the slope), you place them on their inner edges and then move one ski upward at a time, while supporting yourself on the other ski's inner edge and with your poles.

On an even steeper slope, you must bend your knees all the more forward and into the slope.

If the slope is extremely steep, you can sidestep obliquely upward, but keep in mind that the skis must always be straight across the fall line, or else you will glide forward or backward down the slope.

The two-beat diagonal uphill. Lower the upper body forward, but not so much that the ski slips at the kickoff. The angle between pole and snow is more acute than in the two-beat diagonal on a level surface. The easy rhythm used on a level surface should be kept here as long as possible. The steeper the slope, the shorter the pole plants and gliding steps become. Effective uphill movement with the two-beat diagonal requires skis with good grip (either perfectly waxed or waxless skis with sharp patterns) and with a very hard flex.

A The snowplow stop. Move out the tails of the skis by pushing on your heels. At the same time, place them on edge. The more you do this, the faster you will stop. **B** The hockey stop. Swing the skis across the trail. The steeper the slope is, the lower your body position should be. Keep your arms out in front and away from your body, and turn both legs simultaneously in the direction across the trail.

Stopping on skis

To be able to stop or change direction, you must create frictional forces. When you turn for such a purpose, the resultant of these forces is centripetal—directed inward to the center of the turn. This means that you always have to adapt the movement to your body position and use your muscles in a way which counterbalances the centripetal force. If you do not succeed in doing so, you will either fall over or not achieve the turn.

The snowplow

The simplest way of checking speed or stopping is to use the classic snowplow. By bending your legs, with equal pressure on both heels pushing the rear sections of the skis outward, the friction between the angled skis and the snow is increased. If at the same time you move your knees and ankles inward, the inner edges of your skis will further increase the braking effect. You can widen or reduce the angle of the snowplow to regulate your speed. In the narrower "sliding snowplow", the skis are not edged as much as in the wider snowplow stop.

Since the skis are pointing in different directions in the snowplow position, it is easy to change the direction of your forward movement. When you increase the pressure on the inner edge of one ski, it will steer toward the direction it is pointing in as the frictional forces on the snow increase. A good ski will bend under this loading—known as reverse camber—and its flex curve helps you to turn. If the ski has the

"Telemark" waisted form, it will be even easier to turn with. By skiing in a sliding snowplow position down a slope that is smooth and not too steep, you can steer your skis to either side without difficulty. You alternate the pressure on the inner edges and steer with your feet in the desired direction.

The hockey stop

Another effective method of controlling speed is what Alpine skiers call the hockey stop. The initial position is low, with legs well bent and skis wide apart. The arms are held far forward and out to the sides. Let your skis glide downhill so that you gain a fair forward speed. By turning both legs strongly and simultaneously, you will throw the skis across the direction in which you were travelling, so that you come to a stop. It is vital to be supported on your heels the whole time and to maintain the low, almost sitting position.

You can develop this turning movement with both legs at once, and use it in other skiing situations: for example, to execute a sideslip when traversing a slope or even going straight downhill. Instead of turning energetically, you carry out the movement rather gradually and steer the skis gently into the required curve by means of your feet and knees. Remember that the skis slip more easily and are not edged so much in this variant. Modern touring skis with their excellent flex curves and metal edges are almost as easy to maneuver as the Alpine type, particularly if they are complemented by a sufficiently rigid ski boot and good support for the heels.

C Going downhill. *(1)* A skier in the basic position. The feet, knees, and hips are slightly bent. The distance between skis is comfortable for the individual. The arms are relaxed and low. Unevenness of the ground is absorbed by the knees. *(2)* To gain speed, the skier takes up a more forward-leaning position with the poles held against the body and the hands together in front, so as to minimize air resistance. *(3)* To go even faster, the skier lowers his body as much as possible between the thighs. It is especially at the hips and knees that the lowering occurs. This low posture is sometimes called the "egg position".

A wide stance when skiing straight downhill gives better lateral stability. The muscles should be relaxed and you should stand on the whole foot as much as possible.

Downhill skiing

Regardless of whether you are skiing downhill in a trail or on an open slope, the aim here is to achieve a natural, relaxed basic position, ready for any sequence of movement. You stand with your whole foot on the ski, your weight equally distributed, and your ankles, knees, and hips slightly flexed. If you are skiing down a cross-country trail, the distance between your feet will normally be determined for you. In other circumstances, this distance should be such that you can stand comfortably and securely with the entire base of the ski resting on the snow. If you tend to ski on the inner edges (cross-legged and knock-kneed) or outer edges (bow-legged), you should change your basic position—if necessary by inserting orthopedic soles in your boots. Keep your arms slightly bent, with the poles raised forward and a little out to the sides. You are now prepared to cope with the various problems that may appear on the way down.

If you want to go faster, you can assume the *high-speed* position, in which the upper body leans forward, the poles are tucked firmly under the upper arms, and the two hands are held together in front of the body. This attitude gives the skier less wind resistance than in the normal basic stance, but with equally good mobility. The *slow* position involves bending the hips and knees so that the trunk is virtually parallel with the slope, while the hands are held like a plow in front of the face. This position is very tiring over any length of time and requires special practice. A more restful variant on long, even downhill slopes is to let the elbows rest on the thighs.

Humps, hollows, and crossings

If you ski on rough terrain, you are going to encounter hummocks, bumps, and hollows. You can pass these best with an easy, supple leg action, bending and stretching the legs to follow the changing contours. An excellent piece of training is to dig a series of humps and bumps, then try to ski over them by using a two-beat diagonal stride. Another variant occurs when the trail surfaces push the skis alternately and separately up and down. Where abrupt transitions are reached—for example, from steep to more level terrain, or if the skier suddenly comes to thicker or softer snow in front of him—he must be ready to check his forward impetus. The easiest way of dealing with these transitions is to push one foot forward a little and, at the same time, put most weight on the rear ski. The hands should be raised slightly out to the sides for better balance. A deep hollow or a ditch can often be cleared in the same manner.

To traverse a slope, you must ski obliquely across it instead of going straight down the fall line. Lower yourself from the basic position, with bent ankles and knees, leaning your upper body slightly forward and keeping a wide stance. The uphill ski should be a little in front of the downhill ski. The uphill edges of both skis should bite into the snow. The softer the snow is, the less inward the knees need to lean so that the ski edges can bite. The steeper the hill is, the more you must push your hips and knees sideways toward the slope.

The two-beat diagonal on broken terrain. When you reach a hump, you must try to take it as softly as possible. Just before coming to its highest point, bend the knee of your supporting leg to absorb the sudden unevenness. After passing this point, extend the leg forward and downward to retain contact with the snow.

A special technique can be used when you reach a place where one ski track is higher or lower than the other. Training for this is best done by digging a trail with ski tracks as in the diagram below. (1) Here the skier is supported on the right leg, which is descending the peak of a hump, while the left leg moves up another hump. (2) The left leg has now surmounted its hump and the skier begins to shift his weight onto that leg. (3) The left leg is descending the hump and carries the skier's weight, while the right leg has reached the peak of another hump.

Changing direction

Shown in the sequence at right is the step turn. It consists of a series of small sidesteps, made by shifting your weight to one ski while stepping with the other ski. The ski tips are moved mainly, and the tails stay in contact with the snow. Practice the turn also in the other direction until you can turn with equal ease to either left or right.

The skating turn is shown here without poling. The right ski carries the body weight while the left ski is moved over to the new direction. The outer ski is edged and you kick off powerfully with it, at the same time shifting your weight to the inner ski. This is done by leaning into the turn and then moving the outer ski so that it is parallel with the inner ski.

In a prepared cross-country trail you can, as a rule, simply let your skis follow the track. At high speeds, frictional forces increase and you may have problems keeping yourself on the track when it curves. Try to push your outer foot forward and make sure you are resting firmly on your heels. The ski will then be more centrally weighted and you need only tip it slightly on its inner edge in order to follow the trail. To withstand the resultant turning forces, you must lean toward the center of the curve so that the skis are correctly positioned. Sometimes, a good method is to leave the outer ski in the trail if this is icy and fast, and to let the inner ski slide freely on the untracked snow, immediately under your inward-leaning body. You will be skiing with your skis further apart and may feel more stable.

Step turns

On level ground and shallow slopes, the step turn is the easiest way of changing direction on skis and, in certain conditions, it is the best way

of stopping. By lifting one ski at a time and turning the front outward and to the side, you gradually change to the desired direction, or you stop, when the skis have reached a position across the fall line or pointing slightly uphill. This is also an excellent balancing exercise that teaches you mobility and forces you to stand on your skis correctly.

Skating steps

When a ski trail changes direction, it is sometimes useful to shift your weight quickly from one ski to the other by means of a skating action—the ski tips are turned out as in skating. If this is done vigorously and with a quick stretching movement of the outside leg as the trail curves, you can also increase your speed. The effect of the skating turn can be reinforced by double poling as you begin to kick with the outside leg. You can also perform several skating steps in succession, either straight ahead to increase speed, or in a long turn.

Inner-edge turns

When a ski trail is crowded or there is something in the way, you may have to make an abrupt change of direction. You can do this by turning the forward foot slightly inward so that the ski points in the desired direction. The ski tip will be turned in and, as it is moved forward after the completion of the kick, the ski is turned on its inner edge. This maneuver can be executed within the two-beat diagonal rhythm while losing no speed.

Stem turns

On steeper slopes, one may use the snowplow to turn, as already described. But this is not very practical on long slopes with varying snow conditions and perhaps steep descents. It is altogether too laborious to ski in the snowplow position for any length of time. You can instead employ a technique in which you utilize the advantages of the snowplow only at the actual moment of turning, but return to moving on parallel skis between turns. In its simplest form, it is sometimes called the basic turn and is executed in the following manner.

Begin to traverse down a slope that is not too steep. Pressing on both heels, push the tails of the skis outward. Steer the skis downhill in a narrow snowplow position, and gradually shift your weight onto the inner edge of the downhill ski. When the skis start to steer in the new direction, move the uphill ski toward the downhill ski so that they are parallel again. Continue the turn with the skis apart and in a gentle, controlled sideslip forward. You are now ready to execute a new turn, or to continue traversing the slope in the new direction for as long as you wish.

You can also begin a turn by lifting or pressing only the uphill ski into the slope. This is called the *uphill stem*, and results in the ski pointing more or less down the slope in the new direction when you have set it on its inner edge. As you subsequently increase the pressure on this ski, it will steer you around the turn. You will sense a rhythm in carrying out the two-stage movement: first a check, then a transfer of weight, and the turn is completed with a gentle sideslip of the parallel skis. When shifting your weight onto the uphill ski, you may plant the lower pole for support.

In steep terrain and when you have a pack on your back, it may be better to use the *downhill stem*. This is a braking turn which, if correctly executed, helps you to ski down even very steep slopes with rhythm and complete control. By pressing the downhill ski downward and slightly across the direction in which you are skiing, you can check your speed. Sink down by bending your legs a little more, and support yourself by means of the angled lower ski. You will experience a springy, bouncing movement that helps in transferring your weight onto the uphill ski, which is then turned down the slope and set increasingly on its inner edge. Again, it may be useful to support yourself with the downhill pole as the weight transfer is started. You complete the turn with a steered sideslip and parallel skis.

Turning on a prepared ski trail. Move the outer ski forward and stand firmly on your heel. Lean your body into the curve slightly. Edge the outer ski a little. The skis will then follow the trail.

The snowplow turn during a traverse. The secret of this maneuver is that the turn goes in the direction of the weighted ski. Push the ski tails apart to form a plow. Weight one ski (the left ski here) and edge it slightly. Hold your arms a bit outward and your pole tips backward. You will then begin to turn in the direction of the weighted ski.

75

(right) The basic turn. Begin by traversing on a slope that is not too steep. The skis are parallel and the uphill ski is somewhat in front of the downhill ski. Change to a plow position. Increase the pressure on the inner edge of the outer ski. You begin to swing in the direction of the

(above) The stem turn. Traverse in the basic position. Push out the uphill ski's tail so that the ski points in the new direction and is somewhat on its inner edge. Weight both skis equally. When you reach the fall line, you must place more weight on the inner edge of the outer ski, and decrease the pressure on the inner ski while letting it glide inward until it is parallel to the outer ski. The end phase of the turn can be a moderate, controlled sideslip if the terrain is steep or if the surface is icy.

weighted ski. Let the inner ski glide toward the outer ski until both skis are parallel. When they are also lightly edged, they begin to sideslip a little.

The difference between a basic turn and a plow turn is that the former begins and ends with parallel skis.

The uphill stem and the downhill stem are turns in which the skier pushes off with one leg, but the downhill stem involves turning the upper ski in the desired direction.

A Uphill stem. Having started with a normal traverse, you push out the uphill ski's tail so that the ski will point in the direction of the coming turn. This is now the outer ski and, when your weight is next shifted onto its inner edge, the ski will steer you around the turn.

B The downhill stem is good for broken terrain and when you wear a backpack. As you traverse, push out the downhill ski, somewhat across your direction of travel, and set it hard on its inner edge so that it makes a "platform" in the snow. You thus get a braking and rebounding effect which helps you to shift your weight onto the uphill ski, at the same time as you turn it in the desired direction. The weighted ski then steers you around the turn.

77

The Telemark turn

A classic turn, now returning to its place of honor in skiing, is the Telemark. It was originally developed as a way to check speed and stop after running down a slope. At that time, in the nineteenth century, people used quite long skis and normally had only one pole or none at all. The skier could choose simply whether to go to the right or left. Little by little, a technique was evolved whereby several turns could be linked into a flowing sequence. This method is excellent in soft snow and, with practice, is also usable in other conditions.

You assume the starting position for the Telemark by sinking down gently. Let your front foot glide forward and the rear foot backward. Usually most weight goes on the front foot, but you can adapt this emphasis to the snow conditions and the size of the turn. Longitudinal stability is good, while lateral balance can be improved considerably by raising your hands out to the sides a little. Start the turn by angling or turning the leading ski in the required direction at the same time as you edge it a bit by tipping your knee inward. For anatomical reasons, you should have that knee pressed forward over your toes so that the ankle locks and becomes more stable. The rear heel will be raised and the rear knee will point down at the rear ski.

Varying the angle between the skis and shifting the weight forward and backward will help you to steer the turn. Do not sink down too much, or your position may be too firmly fixed. Longer turns are initiated by a progressive transfer of weight onto the front ski, but in soft snow this transfer is not completed. On shorter turns and harder surfaces, the Telemark works better if your edging and weighting are more decisive. You should, of course, use skis with an even flex curve and a pronounced waist: the Telemark form. A series of Telemark turns executed with a sound technique and harmonious movements is as elegant and functional as any modern mode of changing direction.

The Telemark turn is becoming ever more popular again, especially in North America where it can be said to have experienced a real Renaissance. This boom is encouraged by the development of Telemark skis with marked side camber and steel edges. The turn has many advantages: it gives stability in powder snow, and works well when you carry a rucksack, while the position allows the skier to shift his weight back and forth when overcoming humps or hollows.

At the left is shown a perfect Telemark situation: powder snow on a fairly steep slope, with a skier wearing a backpack. How the turn is executed appears at the right. You begin by traversing, and then sink down with bent knees. Let one ski glide forward until its middle is level with the tip of the other ski. Steer by varying the angle between the skis and by shifting your weight.

It is characteristic of the parallel turn that the skis remain parallel during the whole turn. You turn both skis in the desired direction simultaneously. This is made easier by unweighting the skis: your body rises up rhythmically *(1)* and then sinks down *(2)* with a pole plant. Finish the turn by weighting the outer ski more than the inner ski, and execute a short sideslip *(3)* before you get ready for the next parallel turn.

Parallel turns

These are the turns that you perform by simultaneously twisting both skis in the same direction. You will have already executed this movement when practicing the hockey stop. You then experienced a low, almost sitting position, with a good distance between the skis and properly supported on your heels, which made it easier to turn your skis. A rhythmical raising and lowering of the body helps to reduce the pressure of the skis on the surface and facilitates their turning. If you make several of these stretch-and-bend movements, and at the same time turn the skis alternately to right and left, you will execute a sequence of short parallel swings. Each change of direction is completed by a gentle slide before you begin the next turn.

The pace of the bending and stretching movements, and the speed and power with which you turn the skis, determine the radius of turning. Short turns require quick movements, and longer turns need more extended ones. A rhythmical poling action helps a lot, especially on steep slopes and short turns. With a correct hip action, and a finely attuned sense of when you are balanced over the center of the skis, it is quite possible to run downhill on mountain or touring skis, doing parallel turns and carrying a heavy pack. This is simply a matter of adapting yourself in a natural way to the terrain, speed, and snow conditions, without unnecessary or exaggerated movements.

Training trails and loops

As all cross-country skiing should be adapted to external circumstances, it is a good idea to lay out various practice trails in the appropriate terrain. To begin with, an oval or rectangular layout is the best to train on. See that the trail is properly prepared and that it offers good pole grip. This is where you will usually practice the diagonal stride on curves, with inner-edge turns. You may complement the original trail with another which crosses it obliquely, and perhaps a circular one to increase the potential variations for training.

You can next lay out a number of connecting trails and return loops to utilize additional terrain. Long, flat ascents and short, steep hills are needed for training in uphill skiing. Uneven, bumpy trails provide practice in independent leg action, where you must continually adapt your skiing to the terrain. Remember to practice downhill skiing on both the trails and the slopes. Not much imagination is required to devise a range of possibilities. Do not make the loops too long, and keep in mind that the trails should not be too wide if children are going to train there. Skiing in forest country, making your way through the trees on untracked soft snow, increases all-round skiing proficiency. You could also try to build a small jump on a suitable hillside, to train your balance and practice landing in the Telemark position. Make sure that the landing area is on a downhill slope and not on level ground.

Skiing in mountain country

When you ski uphill, you must choose a route that seems as safe and comfortable as possible. It is seldom a good idea to go straight up the fall line, except where a very short, steep slope is involved and the snow conditions are suitable. Generally, you should go obliquely across the slope in long traverses, turning at convenient spots. A common fault occurs when the leader of a group climbs too steeply as his skis grip well on the untracked snow. Those who follow on the trail, which becomes trodden down and hard, experience backslip. A good rule if you are in the lead is to climb without the aid of poles. Then your ascent will usually be only moderately steep.

Turning is sometimes also a problem, especially on a steep slope. Often it is easiest to turn downhill by means of a kick turn, so that you stand with your back to the hill. Thus, if you should fall, you can start with your head up,

rather than down as might be the case if you tried to turn on the slope with your back turned outward. Remember to fix yourself with the poles when you turn, keeping at least three support points always in contact with the surface. This applies to all modes of changing direction when the slope is steep. On an extremely steep ascent, you can side-step your way up. This is a safe method if your skis have good edges. Occasionally, it is simpler to take your skis off, fasten them on your backpack, and continue upward on foot by using your poles.

Do not forget to check all your equipment when the going is steep, so as not to suffer unnecessary losses if any items fall and disappear or break. Should you have to leave behind your equipment—including your skis and perhaps a backpack—for a short time, as when climbing the last part of a summit, choose a place that will be easy to find on the way down, and secure the equipment so that it does not slide or blow away.

All skiing downhill must be done under controlled conditions. Hold yourself in check and ski "defensively". Study the snow in front of you and adapt your technique to the surface. Even on the way up, you can get an idea of the best choice of a route down, and of the prevailing snow conditions. Keep your group together and let some of the best skiers go last, so that they can help anyone in difficulty without having to retrace their steps uphill. Ski in a stable position, taking your weight on the whole foot. In certain snow conditions, it is advantageous to adopt the Telemark position with one foot pushed forward. You could also ski down in long traverses and use kick turns to change direction at safe spots. For short, steep passages it may be best to take off your skis and walk down, secured from above by ropes if necessary. In other places, depending on the snow and terrain, and on your own technical skill, you must choose the most suitable type of turn. The greater your repertory of practiced movements, the better are your prospects for getting the most out of mountain touring and for enjoying the equipment you have selected.

Touring 4

When you have acquired enough of the basic skills of cross-country skiing, and have extended your experience with your equipment, it is time to start applying what you have learned. A short or long tour in the nearest suitable terrain can be just as splendid as an ambitious ski tour somewhere up in the mountains. Only a few inches of snow need have fallen for you to make your first ski tour of the year. Choose open country where the snow accumulates best and the surface is soft—a grassy area or a sparsely forested one is preferable.

The enjoyment of nature with its pure white covering of snow, the surrounding landscape and the often clear air, as well as the physical activity involving your whole body despite the cold, together provide a completely absorbing experience. All trails show up plainly on the ground, and the contours of the earth are rounded and softened. The light changes through different shades of blue, and perhaps there is sunlight to be reflected from the glittering crystals of snow.

A very short ski tour of just a few miles does not demand much special preparation. You can use the same light and convenient equipment, with well-waxed or waxless skis, which served for your first training in basic skills. It is important to wear clothes that allow total freedom of movement, while letting the body get rid of its excess heat and, where necessary, protecting it from heat loss through wind and cold.

Equipment which should be taken with you on a longer day tour. The rucksack has no frame: many people prefer this to a framed rucksack since it keeps the contents closer to the back and is more flexible for the wearer. Personal choice based on experience will help to determine the contents of the rucksack, but the absolutely essential items are shown here.

a warm sweater, to be worn during rest stops. (2) Bandaids for possible blisters. If you feel that a foot is beginning to develop a blister, you should immediately put a bandaid on it. (3) An extra pair of socks. (4) Fruit and food box. (5) Thermos with warm fruit drink or similar beverage. (6) Mat for sitting on. (7) Matches.

(8) Knife. (9) Spare ski tip if the tip of your ski gets broken, you can push the spare on and reach home without too much trouble. If the broken ski is too wide for the spare tip, you can whittle down the ski so that the tip fits. (10) Spare cable if you use a cable binding. (11) Screwdriver for possible repair of bindings.

Day touring

With more experience behind you, and greater self-confidence, it may be desirable to plan for a somewhat longer tour in daytime. This can be considered as a half-day trip or exercise run on prepared trails, perhaps during a skiing weekend at a suitable place in your area. You must, of course, take your own fitness and degree of practice into account, as well as the experience and training of other people who join you. It is nearly always best to go ski touring in company with others, such as your family or friends interested in skiing. For safety reasons alone, you should be with others who can help in an emergency. On long ski tours and when far from habitation, travelling with a few companions is absolutely vital.

Once you have decided where you will go on your tour, study a map of the area to see that appropriate ski trails, paths, and objectives for your excursion are marked. Remember that you may not be able to ski freely wherever you like, and may need to stay in particular sectors: general rights of access do not apply in some countries. If you are not sure that you can read a map, try to obtain a simpler sketch map, which is available for many places with special ski trails. Otherwise, a guide or somebody with local knowledge will tell you what can be found in the area. In many places, too, it is possible to join an organized day tour, on which a ski guide or leader

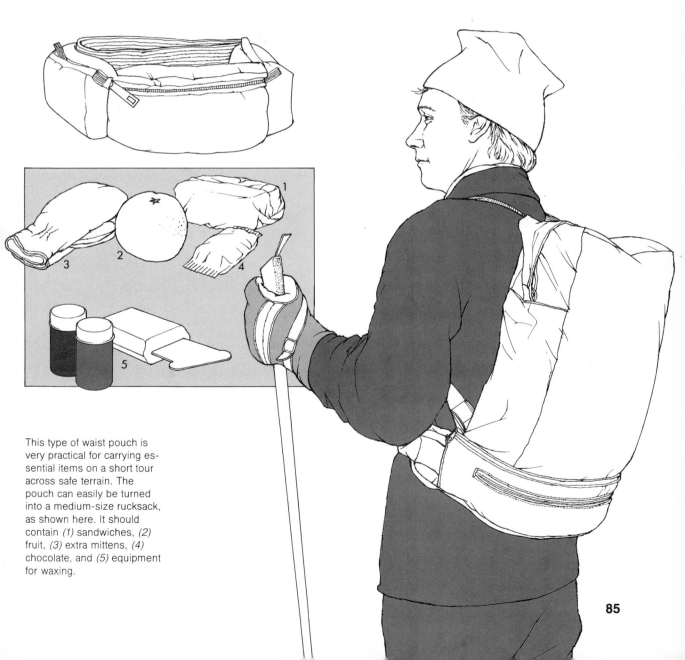

This type of waist pouch is very practical for carrying essential items on a short tour across safe terrain. The pouch can easily be turned into a medium-size rucksack, as shown here. It should contain (1) sandwiches, (2) fruit, (3) extra mittens, (4) chocolate, and (5) equipment for waxing.

helps with the planning and with choosing a good trail for the party. It might be a good idea to avail yourself of some such arrangement if you are going on your first extended ski tour. A map will give you information not only on directions and distances, but also on how strenuous the tour is likely to be. Big differences in elevation naturally make skiing more tiring, since climbing—and even skiing downhill, for many people—can greatly tax untrained muscles.

Even if your tour is going to be only a few miles, it can be valuable to take along some extra gear. Spare clothing such as a thick sweater or a lined jacket is useful for putting on in short breaks or longer rest periods during the day. Something to eat may also be welcome, whether or not you plan to lunch outdoors. A bar of chocolate or a little grape sugar and raisins is often just what the participants require to make the whole tour a success. Similarly, if it is difficult to choose the right skiing wax for the day, take a few extra cans of wax and a scraper, so that you can change wax along the way. The simplest means of carrying these small items is perhaps a jacket or parka with suitable pockets. But if you add a map or sketch of the area, sandwiches and a Thermos bottle, and possibly a compass, knife, and box of matches, you may need a separate holder for them, and a waist pouch or a small backpack is best.

Longer day tours

Longer outings of one whole day demand much more in preparation and equipment. In mountain country, for example, either the distance or the variations in altitude can make touring strenuous and keep you outdoors for a considerable time. You need almost the same items as when taking a trip of several days with overnight stays at cabins or mountain huts. All that you could leave behind for one day would be sleeping equipment and some of the food. Particular requirements are the following.

Substantial clothes for skiing during the daytime, in accordance with the multi-layer principle, allow you to ventilate away any excess heat produced by hard exertion and, at the same time, protect the body against chill and dampness. *Additional garments* serve for rest periods, or if

Cross-country skiing need not require deep snow, great heights, or fashionable clothing and equipment. A frozen lake, or a canal with a thin snow cover, is enough for this boy to learn to appreciate the winter landscape during a short ski tour in the sun.

the weather should worsen, or if you reach a spot—such as the top of a mountain—where wind and cold are extreme. *Further spare clothes* consist of mittens, dry stockings or woolen socks, a peaked balaclava or other warm headgear, and ski goggles. *Safety equipment* such as a bivouac sack, snow shovel, safety rope, matches and wax candle, map, pocket flashlight, and compass, is also essential.

The best place to carry these items is on your back in a fairly large rucksack that fits your own physique. It need not be a pack of the framed type, which is often too big and cumbersome. An Alpine rucksack, preferably of the skiing type that lies close to your back and is specially designed to follow its contours without hampering your movements in skiing, is most suitable. A chest strap or a hip harness may be very useful when you need to relieve the load of the rucksack on your shoulders a little, and to stop the rucksack from swinging out of control when you are skiing—especially downhill.

Food and drink

If you are going to be out all day, you must plan your food and drink very carefully. Many people like to organize their provisions for the day in a cabin and then to supplement these with a hot drink, either from a Thermos or brewed outdoors during a longer break for eating and resting. The drawback of Thermos bottles is that only a rather small amount of liquid can be carried, and you need to drink a lot during a whole day's skiing. Such bottles are also easily broken or damaged, although expensive unbreakable Thermos flasks of steel now exist.

Using a suitable camping stove, you can melt some snow and boil provisions outdoors. A storm-cooker, as it is called, burns either methylated spirit, kerosene, or gas. The gas type is simplest to operate, but has limited usefulness in cold weather. Spirit stoves function better, yet are also sensitive to low temperatures, at which the spirit does not vaporize so easily. These, however, remain the commonest kind of cooker and the most convenient to handle. Kerosene provides better heating, but is more complicated. This stove needs more attention as the kerosene must be preheated with another igniting fluid before gas and light are produced. In addition, it tends to be built rather heavily and to be cumbersome for carrying on short tours.

A hot, sweet soup made of fruit such as bilberry can work wonders for a tired, chilled skier. Hot bouillon or sweet tea is also good for drinking outdoors. The easiest things to eat will be ready-made sandwiches with tasty fillings. Some cooked meat, smoked or cured, is good for slicing, but you should remember that the body is most in need of carbohydrate after exertion.

If you are touring in forest areas, you can readily make a fire to heat food and drink. Be sure to choose a well-sheltered spot and to avoid making the fire bigger than necessary. Use only dry branches and wood from dead trees, and learn to select what burns well. Build up a layer of material on the snow that does not burn so quickly, in order to prevent the fire from disappearing into the snow. Kindle the fire with birch bark and small, dry spruce twigs—then feed it

The storm cooker is the most suitable open-air stove. It has an internal spirit burner and the cooking utensils can be nested in it to save space.

with larger dry wood or, even better, a thick piece of resinous pine which burns nicely. Do not forget to put the fire out properly afterward, and to remove all traces of it and of your presence as far as possible. Whatever you hide in the snow will, of course, come to light in the thaw!

Rest periods

Short halts for purposes such as adjusting clothes, gathering the group together, or enjoying a beautiful view, may be distinguished from longer and somewhat more organized rests. If the tour is as long as three to four hours of skiing, the rest break should last about one hour. It takes a while before the body can recover sufficiently for your strength and judgement to last until they are needed most—at the end of the day's touring.

When taking a long break, you should always put on extra clothing to avoid unnecessary heat loss. Choose a sheltered place, preferably in the sun, within a hollow or among trees or behind boulders. The best shelter from a boulder is often found about 4–5 m (12–16 ft) behind it, not close to it where the wind tends to eddy around. Notice how the wind blows the snow, and take shelter in a calm spot. If there is no natural shelter, do not go without your break, but utilize whatever can be made from your backpack or those of companions, or from a sled which might be stood on end. You could also crawl into a bivouac sack, whose uses will be explained later on.

When you prepare food with a storm cooker or a gas cooker, you should rest it on the undersides of skis. Otherwise there is a risk of the cooker disappearing into the snow when it gets warm. If the methylated spirit is cold and the flame does not light, you can warm the spirit by holding a match to the burner. When the food is ready, let the spirit burn out, or else the protective cap on the burner may loosen and allow unburned spirit to get on the food and clothes in your rucksack while you are skiing.

Even small children can go along on a short ski tour. In a well-insulated sled with protection against the sun, a child can lie warm and happy.

Rest stops during a ski tour are important. This is when you gather your strength for the rest of the tour. On a fine day with little wind, you can set up a wind-shelter by sticking skis into a bivouac sack and standing them in the snow. Next, dig a place for your feet, lay out a mat to sit or lie on, and rest there while you enjoy the view, check your equipment, and have something to eat and drink.

Long tours

A really long tour of a week or more—regardless of whether you want to stay overnight in unmanned rest huts or to camp outdoors—will require a great deal of the participant's physical fitness and skiing ability, the route planning, and the equipment. You must be thoroughly acclimatized to outdoor life and fully at home on skis before you venture on a long tour. The tour should be planned, and perhaps carried out, with experienced companions if you have the chance. Otherwise, you may be able to go on an organized ski tour of several days, arranged by a suitable agency such as a ski touring center or a travel bureau. You would then receive a list of proper equipment in advance, and an appointed leader would be responsible for conducting the tour.

Obviously, the longer your planned trip is, the more equipment you must take along: either on your back in a rucksack, or on a sled towed behind you. Food is particularly heavy and will limit the duration of the tour. Normally, you need about 1 kg (2.2 lb) of food per person per day. To prepare and cook this amount suitably, around 1–

1.5 liters (2–3 pints) of methylated spirit per week are required. If you are used to camping stoves and can utilize them efficiently by cooking in ways that get maximum benefit from the heat, you can greatly reduce fuel consumption. The season and the height above sea level will also affect cooking times and fuel consumption.

Sleeping bags

An overnight kit usually consists of a sleeping bag and mat, sometimes with a sheet bag or an overlay or cover to improve the insulation further. The range of use for a sleeping bag is determined by design factors: its construction, thickness, and amount of insulating material, and whether its filling is man-made or of down. If you are going to sleep indoors in a cabin, you will probably not need a very thick sleeping bag, and a simpler model will do. But overnighting in a snow shelter or a tent is much more demanding. You can obtain a double sleeping bag filled with high-quality down which is sufficient to keep you warm at temperatures down to −25°C (−13°F). The point is to choose a bag that is roomy enough: it is the air inside which maintains your

If the wind is so strong that you cannot set up a bivouac sack on skis, two or three people can crawl into the sack with their rucksacks, after digging a place for their feet to rest.

warmth by conserving heat from your body.

A sheet bag, like those required by youth hostels in many countries, makes the sleeping bag nicer and warmer, as well as easier to keep clean. Washing a soiled sheet bag is far less difficult than cleaning a whole down-filled sleeping bag. Putting a cover over the sleeping bag may be a good idea, both to make it warmer and to protect the thin nylon material from damage by sparks of a campfire or by sharp objects such as branches and twigs. This cover should be loose enough to permit the body's natural breathing, which produces a certain amount of vapour, partly through the skin. Otherwise, you will find that your sleeping bag has become damp on top, perhaps even wet. This reduces the insulating capacity of the bag appreciably and makes it heavier to carry around.

Sleeping mats

However good a sleeping bag you choose, its potential for keeping you warm through the night depends on a really effective sleeping mat. For winter use, you need an insulating layer of about 15–25 mm (0.5–1.0 in) of some synthetic cellular material with sealed air-filled holes separated from each other. The sleeping mat need be no bigger than a generous shoulder-width and shoulder-to-knee length, about 60–75 by 100–120 cm (24–30 by 40–48 in). The clothes you do not need during the night can be placed under your head, and your feet can rest on your empty rucksack.

In Scandinavia many people prefer reindeer skin as a winter sleeping mat. The reindeer has a special kind of hair in its pelt, hollow and filled with air, giving excellent protection against the chilling effect of the snow surface. The best is an untreated skin from a young animal, slaughtered in the fall after summer grazing, when the pelt is dense and the hairs are not too long, so that their usual tendency to drop out or break off is minimized. The skin must be properly cared for, dried after use, and stored in a cool dry place. It is advantageous to treat the inside of the skin with something to prevent damp getting in. A good skin will then give many years of service for overnighting and rest breaks in the snow. A skin can, of course, be cut to the smallest size necessary for comfortable rest and sleep.

The rucksack

Since the equipment on a long tour can become quite extensive, for both the individual and a group, the best way of transporting it must be found. An ample backpack, or rucksack, is still the most usual means of carrying your kit. Any pack should first be tried out by whoever is going to carry it, to make sure that it suits him or her. Often the kit weighs 20–25 kg (40–55 lb) at the start of a long tour, so you may want to use a type of carrying frame with a harness that allows the hips to bear some of the burden. The frame should fit the length of your back, and the lowest strap or hip harness should be level with the lower vertebrae. The hip harness is employed to relieve the shoulder muscles from constantly taking all of the weight. It must sit low enough to pull over the hips and not around the waist, but it should not ride so low that the free movement ot the legs is restricted. Its advantages can be particularly difficult to exploit fully when you are tracking in deep, soft snow and have to lift your legs high.

The rucksack should be roomy enough to hold all necessary items of your kit. Whether you choose a pack divided into sections, or use a smaller pack and supplement this with one or two pouches, is a matter of taste. The total capacity should be 70–80 liters (2.5–3.0 cubic feet), to avoid such tight packing that your kit is hard to reach. An external compartment of some kind is useful for smaller items that need to be kept handy during the day. Addition of outside pockets is easy, and there are packs with detachable pockets or with special attachments for fastening skis.

On a long tour in the mountains, extra equipment is needed in addition to what has already been described as essential for shorter tours. You should also have the safety items which are illustrated on pages 128–129. Shown here are *(1)* an ice saw, *(2)* axe, *(3)* cross-cut saw, *(4)* large snow shovel, *(5)* an avalanche probe which can also be used to measure the depth of snow when you build a snow shelter.

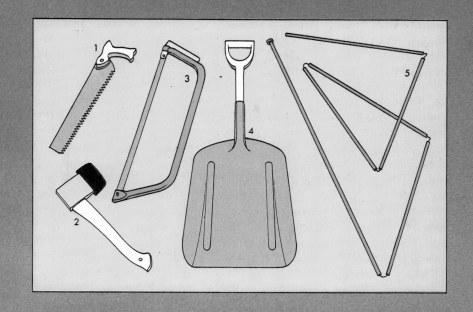

Both the rucksack and its pouches and external pockets should be provided with snow-proof flaps and fastenings to keep out wind-blown snow. All straps, buckles, and laces must be strong enough to stand hard wearing and handling, and be designed for easy opening or closing even by gloved hands. Remember that you may experience very cold weather, which cannot be tolerated by certain plastic and synthetic materials. There is always some relationship between the light weight and practical durability of equipment. Your gear should be as light as possible, but not at the cost of toughness in extreme situations when a safety risk may be involved.

A rucksack should be a large bag that contains a number of smaller ones. Follow a plan when packing your kit, so that in any situation you know where to find the various items. Decide which items should be easily reachable during the day's journey, which safety items might be needed, and what you will want during halts or lunch breaks. The weather may change suddenly, and you must be able to get extra clothing without having to empty your rucksack. When loading and carrying the rucksack, keep in mind that its weight should be minimized and its center of gravity should lie near your back—not too high up, as this could upset your balance when skiing, especially downhill. On a mountain tour, a pack that is too tall and narrow will offer a needlessly large surface for the wind to catch. A large, framed Alpine model is often preferable for skiing in the mountains.

Sled transportation

For many people, a pack of 25–30 kg (55–66 lb), increasing their body weight by 30–50%, is altogether too large a load, particularly on the back. If you cannot reduce your kit, you may instead choose to load it on a sled. A heavy pack can be significantly easier to tow than to carry, on an even surface and across terrain that is not too hilly. However, difficult terrain limits the practicality of a sled, and deep powder snow may make progress almost impossible. When using a sled, therefore, you should study the map carefully and select a route that will minimize differences of altitude. A sled must also be loaded judiciously so that each item of kit has a definite place and is easy to remove when needed.

Although you may be tempted to pack extra items on a sled wherever they can fit, just as in a big rucksack, remember that it is you who are going to pull the sled. Load the sled slightly heavier at the back—an advantage in soft snow—and do not stack items too high as this causes lateral instability. The covering tarpaulin should be of strong synthetic material or cotton, and all straps must be properly fastened. Some sled covers have an opening with a zipper to permit removal of items such as a kit for repairs or first-aid without unpacking the whole sled. It is a good idea to organize your gear into pouches, cardboard boxes, and similar containers.

When pulling a sled in trackless terrain, one or more skiers without sleds should go first, to make what is called a three-track trail instead of the usual narrower kind. This will be wide enough for the sled to be pulled without catching on the snow at the sides. On long ascents, and when

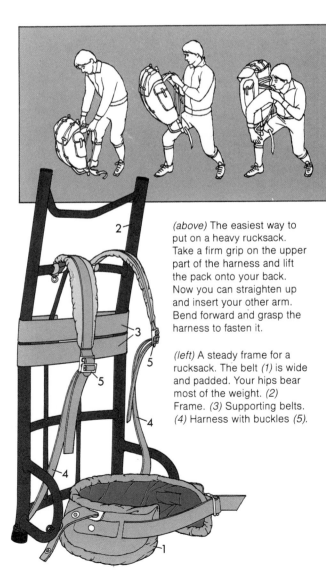

(above) The easiest way to put on a heavy rucksack. Take a firm grip on the upper part of the harness and lift the pack onto your back. Now you can straighten up and insert your other arm. Bend forward and grasp the harness to fasten it.

(left) A steady frame for a rucksack. The belt (1) is wide and padded. Your hips bear most of the weight. (2) Frame. (3) Supporting belts. (4) Harness with buckles (5).

the sled is heavily laden, two skiers may be needed to move it. The one in front pulls by means of a harness around his hips and two strong lines of equal length fitted with loops or sizeable snap-hooks at their ends. These lines are arranged crosswise for an even pull, and are hooked onto the sled's drawgear or the rear skier's harness. For skiing downhill, the front skier's lines can easily be uncoupled and, if necessary, one of them can be attached to the rear of the sled—which should have some kind of fastening—for braking.

Check the sled thoroughly before using it on a long tour, to see that every detail is in order. Reinforce any weak points, especially where the stress is greatest: for example, at the attachments of towing gear. Wax the lower surfaces and repair any holes or other damage. A wooden sled should be impregnated with wood tar and then treated with glide wax for easy running. A synthetic sled can be treated with downhill wax to make it easier to pull.

Clothing

We have already mentioned the various items of clothing that everyone should take on a skiing tour. It is useful and interesting to examine this subject further. Natural fibers like cotton and wool are still popular alongside the synthetic fibers which increasingly occur in modern leisure clothing. A drawback of natural fibers is their price in relation to quality and durability. On the other hand, wool fiber can absorb up to 33% of its own weight in moisture without feeling wet or even damp, and at the same time it retains about 60% of its insulating properties. The type of un-

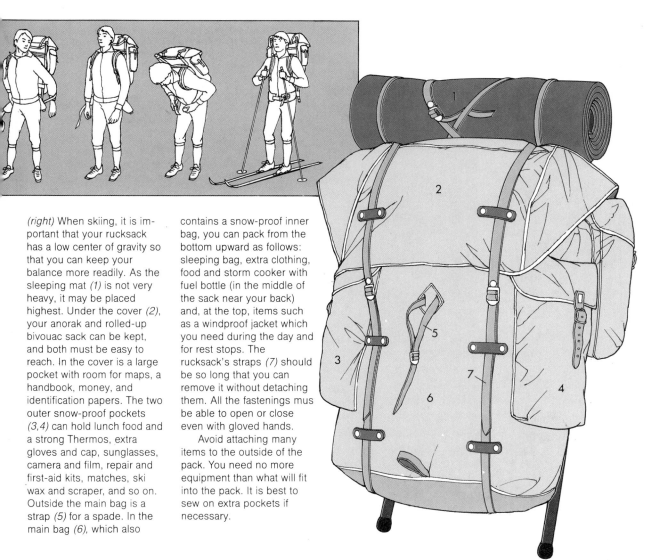

(right) When skiing, it is important that your rucksack has a low center of gravity so that you can keep your balance more readily. As the sleeping mat *(1)* is not very heavy, it may be placed highest. Under the cover *(2)*, your anorak and rolled-up bivouac sack can be kept, and both must be easy to reach. In the cover is a large pocket with room for maps, a handbook, money, and identification papers. The two outer snow-proof pockets *(3,4)* can hold lunch food and a strong Thermos, extra gloves and cap, sunglasses, camera and film, repair and first-aid kits, matches, ski wax and scraper, and so on. Outside the main bag is a strap *(5)* for a spade. In the main bag *(6)*, which also contains a snow-proof inner bag, you can pack from the bottom upward as follows: sleeping bag, extra clothing, food and storm cooker with fuel bottle (in the middle of the sack near your back) and, at the top, items such as a windproof jacket which you need during the day and for rest stops. The rucksack's straps *(7)* should be so long that you can remove it without detaching them. All the fastenings must be able to open or close even with gloved hands.

Avoid attaching many items to the outside of the pack. You need no more equipment than what will fit into the pack. It is best to sew on extra pockets if necessary.

Dress for cross-country skiing so that you become neither cold nor too warm and sweaty. The multi-layer principle (several layers of clothing) is important because it keeps a lot of air in and between the layers. (1) A thin woolen sweater, long underwear, windproof underpants, and long woolen socks. (2) The shirt or vest should be long and made of cotton flannel. Trousers of the "knickers" type are usual. (3) The outermost garments are a windproof anorak, woolen cap, mittens, and ski boots. (4) Lighter touring boots with a low ankle. (5) Strong boots for mountain touring. (6) Mountain boots with inner shoes are extra warm and very practical in overnight cabins, where the shoes can be used as slippers.

derwear that leads the leisure market today, with properties which include removing all moisture from the skin, will work up to a point and need regular washing after each use—otherwise, salts and impurities remain between the fibers, affecting the insulating layer of air. Wearing this type of clothing next to your skin should, therefore, be confined to training runs and short ski tours.

According to the multi-layer principle, several thin layers are better than one thick layer. It is the amount of air enclosed between the layers that provides insulation, since air is a poor conductor of heat. If your multi-layer clothing is pressed together, for example by a strong wind, the insulating effect is much poorer, so at least one layer must be rigid enough to retain its air envelope even in extreme situations. The innermost layer should insulate and, moreover, carry away the moisture that accumulates during extensive hard muscular effort, when excess heat is continually produced. The middle layer should partly absorb the moisture and partly transport it away from the body, while also providing insulation and warmth with an air layer between the inner and outer garments. The outer layer should prevent moisture and cold from penetrating to

In bad weather with driving snow, a long anorak with a hood and windproof trousers will be very useful. Gaiters cover the ankles and boots. Substantial ski goggles make it easier to see in driving snow.

Woolen mittens should have long cuffs and substantial room, preferably for inner gloves. (1) A mitten which is open at the palm and thumb base allows you to free the thumb and fingers when necessary (2), as in preparing food or fixing a binding. (3) The same effect can be obtained by cutting off the tips of an old glove.

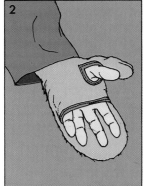

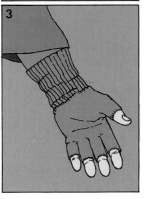

the body, and prevent condensation by letting out some of the moisture from the body.

The best material next to the skin is thin, soft, pure wool of high quality, or perhaps a mixture of such wool with artificial fiber to give better wear. A suitable material for the middle layers can be a strong cotton fabric, possibly augmented by a woolen sweater or waistcoat. Indeed, a thin woolen sweater is almost as warm as a thick one but takes up much less room in your rucksack if you are not using it. Two thin sweaters are more practicable than a thick, heavy one. Many ski tourers today use synthetic fur sweaters, which

are very durable. The outer layer should be of silicon-impregnated, close-weave, tough cotton, perhaps mixed with synthetic fiber for better wear.

As the outer garments are worn on top of your other clothes, they should have roomy pockets and openings that enable you to reach the inner layers but are also easy to close when bad weather begins. All the garments should allow complete freedom of movement, and must be large enough to fit over each other for multi-layering. Thus, even a big quilted or duvet jacket should be wearable under the windproof layer without difficulty. The same applies to wearing quilted trousers inside windproofs and, if necessary, snow gaiters.

There is no need for any highly specialized garments on long ski tours, except for anoraks and windproof pants. These functional items have been developed from Eskimo dress, tested under extreme conditions in a demanding environment. Your windproof anorak should have a hood that will cover your whole head, lacing up or otherwise closing over your face. For additional protection against strong winds and driving snow, the edge of the hood can be trimmed with fur. The best is fur from animals that live in Arctic conditions, such as the wolf and wolverine, although these animals are threatened with extinction and it would be appropriate to substitute dog fur. Your anorak should also be roomy and of adequate length, reaching the knees and cut rather longer at the back than in front, so that it does not pull up when you lean forward or sit. Windproof pants, in the same material as the anorak, should fit easily over your ski boots. Both the anorak and the pants must lace up properly, offering minimal surface for the wind to catch and inhibit movement.

Opinions vary as to the choice of color for outer garments. Dull colors can readily merge with the surroundings and become a safety hazard when you are looking for someone in bad weather. Warm colors like orange, red, and yellow show up well even in poor visibility, but skiers should use them with discretion so as not to be too conspicuous in the natural environment which is visited.

An important supplementary item is a good skiing cap, preferably with extra protection for the forehead, ears, and neck. A peak on the cap will help to hold your anorak hood in place, and out of your eyes so that it does not obstruct your view. The value of keeping your head warm is obvious. Adequate ski goggles, ideally with lenses that are double or non-misting, protect your face as well as allowing you to see in driving snow. For your hands, the most suitable cover is an ample outer mitten over a warm inner mitten. The shank should be long so that there is no gap around the wrist, which is vulnerable to cold.

Rests on long tours

When you are making long trips on skis, perhaps carrying a heavy pack as well, it is best to divide your efforts with regular breaks. The usual way is to ski for 40–45 minutes, then rest for 10–15

A shelter made of snow blocks gives simple and good protection from wind during rest stops. *(1)* Cut out a number of snow blocks across the wind direction. Let the blocks stand and freeze while *(2)* you dig a bench and make a trench for your feet. The bench will be more comfortable for sitting if it is sloped inward at the legs. Raise the blocks on end. *(3)* Spread out a mat to sit on. *(4)* The snow shelter is finished. The cooking area is within comfortable reach.

minutes. With any such interval, everyone in the group needs to know how long the break will last, and that it is timed from the arrival of the last member at the appointed place.

The shorter breaks may involve simply taking your rucksack off your shoulders for a few minutes while you adjust your clothes to avoid unnecessary sweating or cooling down. The choice of location for a short halt will not be critical, but it should provide a sheltered place where wind and driving snow are not too troublesome. A longer pause of more than five minutes, however, means putting on more clothes so as not to lose body heat. This also offers an opportunity for a little hot drink from a Thermos, and for a snack such as chocolate or raisins. Here it is important to select a sheltered spot out of the weather, enabling you to sit down and rest. Equipment can be adjusted if necessary, and anyone who is beginning to get chapped may be attended to.

In the middle of the day, there should be a more generous stop to allow for rest and something substantial to eat. This midday break should last for at least an hour, preferably longer if the day's journey is long and the weather per-

Bivouac sacks

The bivouac sack, or bivvy bag, is one of the most important and useful items of ski-touring equipment. It should go in your rucksack even on the shortest day trip, whatever the weather at the start. Anyone will agree who has sat in a warm, comfortable bivouac sack and heard a blizzard raging outside while, with his gloves off, he sorts through his equipment, changes some clothes, or eats and drinks before continuing his journey.

A bivouac sack is simply a large bag, big enough to accommodate two or three adults, including their rucksacks. Its material should be close-woven so as to keep out the wind, but should let out the moisture from exhaled air and warm bodies so that there is no condensation. Close-weave cotton is best, perhaps mixed with artificial fiber for better wear. The seams must be double, strong, and reinforced at the corners. A bivouac sack should be long enough for a full-grown person to be able to pull it over his head and still be covered down to his feet. The frame should be triangular so that the sack is widest at the bottom. A ventilation hole must exist and is also useful for studying the surroundings without having to go outside. Nylon bivouac sacks are light and moisture-repellent, but unpleasant to stay in during rough weather as the material rattles in the wind. Cotton materials are definitely preferable for winter use. You could, of course, economize by making your own bivouac sack.

The sack should be set up so that minimal area is exposed to the wind, and it is thus best to have one support toward the wind. Dig a trench for your feet, wide and deep enough for everyone to be a little lower in relation to the snow surface and sit rather comfortably. Use an insulating foam-pad sleeping mat and a couple of skis to sit on. Pull the sleeping mat up around your back and place your rucksack and your feet on it. Remember to brush all the snow from your clothes, boots, and equipment: otherwise, you will soon become damp or even wet when the temperature inside the bivouac sack rises above the freezing point. If necessary, change clothes so that you have dry ones next to your skin, and put the damp ones on top, if you expect to stay long in the bivouac sack. Put on extra clothes in the usual manner before you start to feel cold.

A wall of snow blocks on the windward side is to be recommended. Place it 4–5 m (12–16 ft) from the trench you have dug, so that the snow does not drift around the bivouac sack. Anchor

mits. It may be necessary to build a snow-block shelter for proper protection. Put on extra clothes, take out snow shovels or other digging tools, and start immediately to cut a suitable number of snow blocks, leaving them for a while to stand and freeze firm. Dig a straight trench at right angles to—or obliquely with the tip toward—the direction of the wind, so that everyone is sheltered by the snow. Make a broad "bench" big enough for the whole party, and spread out reindeer skins or sleeping mats. Choose a spot for cooking the food if you have the necessary equipment. Place the snow blocks to keep out the wind while you eat, drink, and rest.

Enjoy the landscape and gather your strength before continuing your trek. See that everyone eats sufficiently and help the most tired members of the group. Decide in good time when you should break camp, and ensure that everyone gets ready together. If the weather is bad, you may have to use bivouac sacks and it will be absolutely essential for everyone to leave at the same time. Keep your extra clothes on for the first five minutes of your resumed journey, especially if it is cold and windy.

skis, poles, and other equipment securely in the snow outside, to prevent them from blowing away or getting snowed under. It is unwise to use skis or poles for holding up your bivouac sack, as they are liable to tear the material if the wind is strong. Just pull the sack up over your heads, sit on the sleeping mat and part of the sack, pull in your feet, and lace up the sack at the bottom with the drawstring that should be there. If you have a spirit stove, you can prepare food inside a bivouac sack, but you must be very careful and ensure proper ventilation. Ready-made sandwiches and a Thermos of hot drink are much more convenient.

A bivouac sack is an unequalled and reliable aid when skiers become chilled or fatigued, or in other emergencies. It is one that nobody would want to be without on long ski tours. The sack weighs only about 0.5 kg (or 1 lb), and is no bigger than a Thermos when rolled up, so there is little advantage in leaving it behind. You can also use it to drag away snow while digging a shelter, and it can be set up inside the shelter for additional warmth. One sack for every two people in the group is a more practical arrangement than a smaller number of sacks holding four people each.

Staying overnight

A tour lasting from one day to the next, by either choice or necessity, requires a decision about how and where to spend the night in a snowy environment as conveniently and enjoyably as possible. There are several standard methods, involving different degrees of foresight and effort.

Camping out

You may often want to pitch camp where no built cabin exists. On other occasions, you may not have enough time or suitable conditions to make a snow shelter. A good mountaineering tent is one alternative. Before trying it under winter conditions, you should be very familiar with camping in the mountains at other times of the year. The best tents are the self-supporting tunnel or dome types, which must be of the double-skinned variety. See that the distance between the cloths of the inner and outer tents is fairly large, and preferably choose a model with the cloths stitched together. The inner tent should be of cotton weave so that it can "breathe" and absorb some of the condensation, while the outer cloth should be of strong, close-weave nylon.

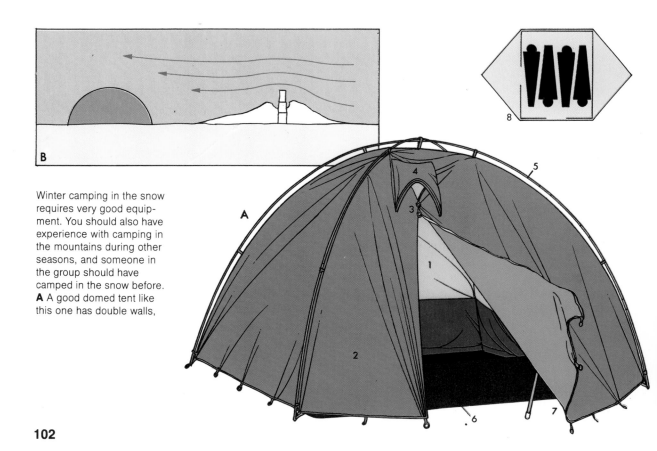

Winter camping in the snow requires very good equipment. You should also have experience with camping in the mountains during other seasons, and someone in the group should have camped in the snow before.
A A good domed tent like this one has double walls,

Select a spot with as much shelter as possible, and shovel away all the soft snow. You can dig right down to the ground if there is not too much snow and the surface is reasonably smooth and level. Otherwise, tread down the surface with your skis to make a firm place for pitching your tent. Dig a trench big enough to avoid any danger of the snow drifting over and burying the tent. If the site is very exposed to the weather, you can build a wall of snow blocks around the tent, or just on the windward side, a little distance away to reduce the effects of wind. But keep in mind that the wind may change during the night.

Anchor all the guy ropes securely in the snow. Use special snow-holding tent pegs, long and made of rough wood or light metal, or what are sometimes called snow anchors. You can also utilize skis, poles, snow shovels, and other equipment for this purpose if necessary. Dig a shallow trench parallel to the side of the tent, and place one ski in it. Fasten one or more guys to the ski, then shovel the snow over it and tread down thoroughly. This will give you a very strong anchorage for the tent. Snow "valances" along the bottom edges of the outer tent are another excellent aid and can be sewed onto your tent.

When covered with snow, they help to hold down the lower part of the tent. However, some circulation of air between the two skins of the tent is essential to prevent much condensation.

Inside the tent, the temperature will not be many degrees warmer than outside, but there will be no wind, and the heat from cooking as well as from the occupants is preserved. Together with a warm sleeping bag and a good insulating mat, the experience can be very pleasant. Still, you should keep the tent properly aired, and avoid steam or fumes inside by cooking food either in the tent porch or entirely outside. If the air in the tent feels chilly and damp, light a stearin candle for a while to give both brightness and warmth. Be careful not to bring in snow when you crawl into the tent, as the snow would soon melt and cause discomfort. Change into dry clothes next to your skin and put on the damp clothes over these. The latter can be partly dried in your sleeping bag during the night by means of the warmth your body produces. Take your ski boots with you into the bottom of the sleeping bag so that they can be put on in the morning, for otherwise they will freeze stiff.

Prepare your breakfast during the previous evening, and remember that it may be impossi-

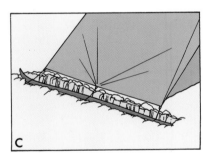

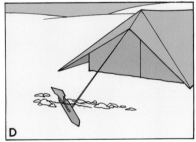

with a fully ventilated inner tent and an outer tent that is completely watertight. Condensation is one of the biggest problems of winter camping, so ventilation is very important. (1) Inner tent. (2) Outer tent. These are sewn together with an ample distance between the cloths.

(3) A two-way zipper can be opened at the top for ventilating the tent. (4) A self-bracing ventilator. (5) Fiberglass frames. (6) The inner tent's bottom is sewn up to form a box. (7) Apse at both sides. (8) This tent is a Fjällräven Termo Camp 78 with room for four people

(3.6 square meters, or 38 square feet, of living area).
B A shelter made of snow blocks will lessen the wind strength around the tent.
C The skis can be used to anchor the guy lines of the tent. But keep in mind that this will prevent you from skiing while the tent is up!

D A broad, long tent peg of wood holds the guy ropes in place.
E A tunnel tent that is well dug in. The tent top is stretched up while you take the equipment inside and brush off your clothes.

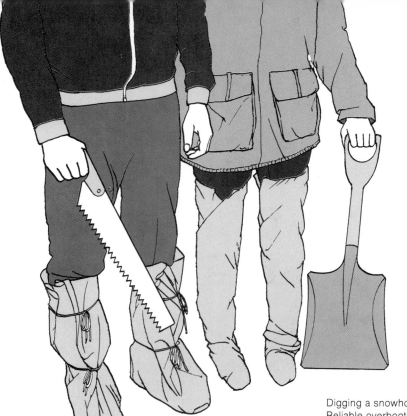

Digging a snowhole in a drift. Reliable overboots or snow gaiters are necessary. The working tool should be an ice saw or an ample snow shovel. A smaller profiled spade should then be used to round off the inside of the roof. *(1)* When you have chosen a drift which is high and deep enough, dig out a trench in the drift so that you

ble in the morning to go out and recover forgotten equipment if the weather has changed during the night. In any conditions, it is much more comfortable to lie in your warm sleeping bag with a hot drink before getting up and continuing your tour. Another good idea is to fill a Thermos with something hot before you retire, so as to have it handy if you wake up cold in the night.

Snow shelters

If you have the right equipment, a planned overnight stay in the snow is a wonderful way of sleeping outdoors. By choosing a good spot and carefully building a temporary snow dwelling, you can easily use this for several nights. Study the map and the surrounding terrain, to decide where large accumulations of snow will probably occur which are suitable for burrowing into. The wind blows quantities of snow into small ravines, along stream valleys, behind raised ground, and into hollows. If you know which way the prevailing winds blow, the slopes with much drifted snow can be located quickly.

A snowdrift of moderate height is your best choice. Consider the risk of an avalanche before you check the thickness of the snow with a probe or ski pole. A depth of 3–4 m (10–13 ft) horizontally into the drift, and a height of at least 2 m (6.5 ft), will give you sufficient room. The snow should have a firm but not icy consistency so that digging is easy. Any soft snow on the surface should be shoveled away and not included in your measurements when assessing a suitable site. It is worthwhile making an extra search to find a good snowdrift before you begin the actual work of digging. Often it is easiest to locate a fine spot down around the treeline, although nothing may prevent you from digging a snow shelter high on the open mountainside.

Prepare for work, making an appropriate division of labor. Everyone must be active and occupied: this is especially important if the weather is cold and windy. Digging from a position high up the snowdrift or slope, so that you need only shovel the snow outward and downward, is least strenuous. One person should dig the loose snow out, a second should shovel it away, and a third must attend to the sled or skis while perhaps heating a drink for all members of the party. If necessary, set up a bivouac sack for additional shelter.

Large and small snow shovels, an ice saw, and

have full standing height and a little more. Meanwhile, another member of the group cuts out a number of snow blocks and leaves them to freeze. *(2)* After dig-

ging in about 4 m (13 ft), begin to hollow out the sides until you have a place to lie along each side, about 2.5 m (8 ft) long and 1.5 m (5 ft) wide, so that you have room

for your rucksack and avoid lying against the snow. *(3)* Stand a snow block on end at each side of the entrance and then build, block by block, until the shelter is

completely covered. Push in a ski pole to make a ventilation hole. *(4)* Cover the structure with loose snow and finally set up a block to serve as a door.

a probe are required. As you can soon get wet when digging in snow, this should be avoided by adapting your clothing if possible. Many people prefer to use foot muffs as protection for their feet and boots, together with rubber gloves. Good snow gaiters and substantial outer mittens generally work just as well. Anoraks and windproof pants are fine, as they keep out the external damp. Do not wear too much clothing under your anorak, since digging is strenuous work and soon makes you sweat. Dig calmly and methodically, changing places frequently with other diggers. Everyone should lend a hand and avoid hurrying. You will take two to three hours, depending on the consistency of the snow, before your shelter is ready for moving in.

Snowhole in a drift

This is a well-tried type of shelter which you dig in the upper edge of a snowdrift. Check the depth of the snow and then dig a small trench straight in, just wide enough to work in with reasonable comfort, remembering that the opening will be closed again later. Dig out the trench high enough for you to stand in, and long enough to allow two platforms for sleeping bags on each

side of the trench. It is best to keep the roof open during the work, since this improves the air circulation and avoids warming the interior. If you make it more cave-like, the temperature rises and the snow sticks to your clothes, so that you are more likely to get wet.

Dig out the complete snowhole and get it ready inside before you roof it over and close the entrance with snow blocks. Preparation of these blocks should be started at the same time as the digging. Let one of the group look for a spot with firm, compact snow, preferably above the drift near the site where you are digging, and use an ice saw to cut out a suitable number of blocks about 1 m (40 in) long, 0.5 m (20 in) high, and 0.25 m (10 in) thick. If you stand them on end for a while, they will freeze better and be ready for use by the time the digging is finished. Make a few spare blocks and keep in mind that you will need a door.

If the blocks have been made higher up the drift, it will be easier to drag or carry them to the roof opening. Be careful not to stamp through the roof. Cut out a niche for the bottom block and determine the height of the opening. Before going further, it is simplest to take inside all the

A snow cave takes about as much time to build as a snowhole in a drift—about two hours when the weather is good. It is preferable to build a snow cave if the drift is not very deep and you come upon either bare ground or hard snow. The building process is then as shown here. Work goes fastest if two entrances are dug at the same time.

equipment you need. If you make the bottom of the trench slope down toward the entrance, and have the sleeping platforms higher than the entrance, you will retain a pocket of warm air that makes the snowhole more pleasant, and heavy gases like carbon monoxide and dioxide from the cooking and breathing will flow away down the sloping floor. Now pile the rest of the snow blocks in position. Fill any cracks with soft snow, and your dwelling is ready.

Various types of door are illustrated here. The roof and walls should be at least 30 cm (12 in) thick, and curved so as to last better. Smooth off any irregularities in wall and roof surfaces, as these would drip when the temperature starts to rise. A profiled aluminum shovel is excellent for doing this. The most agreeable temperature is just a few degrees above freezing, and one or two candles will give quite enough heat and a cozy light. A small snowhole does not necessarily get any warmer than a large one, but the latter is undoubtedly more comfortable. Make the sleeping platforms sufficiently roomy and the roof high enough, so that you do not knock against the snow when you sit up or stand between the bunks.

Keep your equipment neat and tidy, stacking the skis and poles outside the entrance. Do not forget to take a shovel into the snowhole with you for emergencies. It is a good idea to mark the limits of your shelter in the drift above: then you will not have visitors dropping in suddenly through the roof.

Change into dry clothes next to your skin, and put on extra garments. Make a place for the spirit stove, check that the ventilation is adequate, and

prepare your meal. All cooking should be done with the door block open and near the ventilation hole. Keep things as comfortable as possible for yourself and your companions, and recover your strength for the morning. Eat and drink a lot and get yourself ready for the next day's journey. Get into your sleeping bag, but do not wear too many clothes—it is better to put more on later, if you need them, than to perspire much in a narrow sleeping bag. Take your boots inside with you, as well as anything you want to dry.

Snow caves
Another suitable form of snow shelter, the snow cave, is also best dug in the top edge of a snowdrift. This may be easier than the previous type if the wind is strong and the whirling snow makes it hard to dig a trench. Mark out two entrance holes at the same height from the top edge of the drift and about 1.5 m (5 ft) apart. Dig

A When you have found an adequate drift by sounding it with your probe, dig two holes into it. The holes should be as small and low as possible, and separated by about 1.5 m (5 ft). Dig them high enough in the drift to let the excavated snow fall away. This makes your work easier, especially since the uppermost layers of snow are not as hard-packed as the lower ones.

(1) View from front.
(2) View from above.
B Dig in about 1 m (3 ft) and then guide the holes sideways until they meet. Hollow out the space around you as you proceed, so that you have room to work in.
(1) View from front.
(2) View from above.
C Dig out the space to make a bench for lying on. Block up the hole entrance that will not be used as a doorway.

Hollow out a table and a cooking area in the passage between the holes. Make a ventilation opening above the cooking area. Make storage shelves along the short sides of the cave. Even out the roof with a profiled spade so that there are no dripping points. *(1)* View from front.
(2) View from above.
D The snow cave is now ready. A block lies in front of the door. It can be difficult to

raise the door block from inside the cave, and a good method is to drive a ski pole through the block so that its basket is on the outer side: you can then easily lift the block by pulling on the pole handle. A "sliding door" can also be made by placing a snow block on a ski laid across the opening, and the block can easily be moved aside. *(1)* View from side.
(2) View from above.

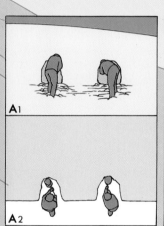

A1

A2

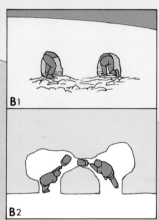

B1

B2

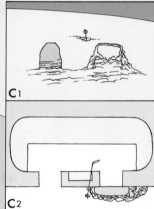

C1

C2

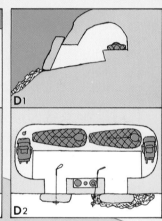

D1

D2

straight in for at least 1 m (40 in) and then at an angle so that the two tunnels meet. Try not to make the entrance holes too big, as they must be covered later. Enlarge the chamber to allow the required number of sleeping places, with room for equipment, cooking, and so on. It is best to make one tunnel high enough to stand up in, and to block the other. Make the roof dome-shaped and cut out niches or shelves according to your needs. Do not forget the ventilation hole and the sloping floor. Carry your sleeping kit inside, and close the entrance either by using a block as a door or by draping a bivouac sack.

Excavating this kind of shelter is warmer work as the air circulation is poor, and there is a greater risk that you will end up soaking wet. Work calmly and methodically, changing diggers frequently. Good use can be made of a bivouac sack to drag out the snow that must be removed: pulling is less strenuous than carrying. As for settling into

the snow cave, you and your companions should proceed as with the previous type of shelter. Leave no equipment outside, and get ready for the morning journey.

Igloos

This type of shelter was, of course, invented by the Eskimos, who used it as a permanent winter dwelling and built it to whatever size they needed. A practical abode, it could easily be abandoned and rebuilt according to the changes in hunting and fishing which made people move onward, and the building material could be found virtually everywhere.

An igloo is advisable when you cannot find a suitable snowdrift for shelter or when the snow cover is not thick enough. The snow should be really firm and hard, as it is then easier to cut out proper blocks. Old, rather fine-grained snow compacted by the wind is best. Choose a smooth surface and brush away any soft snow from it. Use your poles to measure a circle about 3 m (10 ft) in diameter. Remember that the snow blocks will be stronger if allowed to stand on end and freeze awhile.

Place the blocks on end around the circle so that they lean inward. Next, cut down the blocks so that the whole of this first course describes a rising spiral. Bevel the top edges so that the upper surface, if extended, would point toward the opposite wall's base. Ideally, one person should stand inside the igloo and the others outside, organized so that two are building while the rest cut and carry new blocks. Continue to build around in this rising spiral form, leaning all the blocks inward so that they support one another and the opening at the top decreases. Finally, there will be just a small hole on top, which is filled in by a roof block. The person standing inside the igloo is now shut in and must dig his way out.

Mark an entrance on the lee side of the igloo. You may want to build a covered entrance in the form of a tunnel. Dig out sleeping places and a floor inside the igloo, making the chamber large enough for standing room. Take in your equipment, see that there is good ventilation, and then shovel soft snow over the whole structure to seal it against the weather.

It requires a great deal of practice in order to build a solid igloo in reasonable time. But this achievement is immensely satisfying—as is overnighting in a kind of shelter evolved long ago by people native to such an environment.

Cabins and mountain huts

In many touring areas in forest and mountain country, overnight cabins have been built at suitable places, usually at intervals of an average day's journey. These cabins may be relatively simple in furnishings, but there are also better-equipped and more comfortable ones. Some are manned by a warden for part of the year, while others are always open and unsupervised. Usually the cabins lie along a ski route, or where several routes meet or diverge. Occasionally, a hut is located so as to facilitate ascents of an especially attractive mountain group.

What all cabins have in common is their simple and functional overnight accommodation for weary skiers, normally with the chance to cook food indoors. If there is a warden, his or her directions should naturally be followed. Otherwise, the golden rule is that you should leave the cabin in the condition you would wish to find it in. See that there is enough wood, as well as water, for your own and other guests' needs. Do not spread yourself and your equipment all over the place, as it might become crowded. Do not tread snow over the floor and make it unnecessarily wet and unpleasant: brush snow off your feet and equipment before going in. Choose a sleeping place and keep your belongings together there. You may have to share a bunk with a companion or sleep on the floor if it is crowded.

Change into dry clothes and, if you can, dry any that are wet. Chop enough wood for the whole night, if necessary, and bring in water or melt snow for the cooking and drinks. Remember that a group which has been out skiing for the whole day requires a lot of fluid. Light a moderate fire, keep an even temperature, and be prompt to air the damp atmosphere which often develops when a number of people are drying their clothes and cooking. Cook in turn, and let everyone in the cabin have an opportunity to use the stove. Offer spare food to other guests, and remember that those who arrive last—or late at night—will certainly appreciate a mug of hot tea or soup, being much more tired than you are by that time.

Choose a place with firm snow. Mark out a circle by using your ski poles, and trample down the surface. You will need 40–50 snow blocks, each about 40 by 80 cm and 25 cm thick (16 by 32 by 10 inches). Lean the

blocks inward 15° or so from the beginning. The whole first course should form a counterclockwise rising spiral. Bevel the edges with an ice saw so that the blocks join together.

An unwritten rule is that a cabin can never be full, and that there is always room for any skier who wants to stay.

In general, cabins are equipped only for short stays of one or two nights and should not be used for week-long visits. If you have slept for one night on a bunk, give it to any new guests for the following night. You should leave a cabin supplied with chopped firewood and kindling, so that subsequent guests can warm the place up quickly on arrival. On the other hand, you should not leave water inside, as it may well freeze if the cabin is unused for several days in winter. Clean up properly after your visit, sweep the floor, and dispose of any rubbish: put it in the place provided, or take it home with you.

Some of the staffed cabins are able to serve simple meals, and some enable you to replenish your stock of provisions before continuing your tour. Other types of shelters and cabins—and conical huts of the Lapp variety, at some places in Scandinavia—offer simpler overnight accommodation with no bunks and not always the possibility of lighting a fire. Nevertheless, it is occasionally more practical to stay for the night in one of these than to camp out or build a snow shelter. Your overnight kit, sleeping bag, and insulating mat must be of good quality and you must have cooking equipment with you, including fuel.

Base camps

A good alternative to carrying a heavy rucksack every day on a long tour is to set up a base camp and to transport all the necessary equipment and food there. Shorter day trips can then be made with light backpacks containing only the minimum of items. Choose an attractive position for your base camp—well sheltered and, if possible, with access to running water in a stream unless the weather is so cold that it is frozen over. The camp should be in such a position that it makes a good starting point for day tours in several directions.

Transportation to the base camp is best provided by sled and rucksacks. A number of trips may be necessary in order to get everything you need for a long, comfortable stay. A solid and roomy snow cave or igloo can then be built, or tents can be erected. All the hard work involved in transporting the gear to the base camp will prove its value when you are able to go on shorter treks with light packs. Another advantage of the base camp is that you can quickly get back to it if the weather becomes bad and that, when the weather improves, you can start off again with little delay since you need not break camp. Moreover, if the group is big, one or more of the less proficient skiers—or someone who has a minor injury—may need to rest for a day.

Thus, the base camp gives many possibilities for adapting the activities of individuals or a group according to the circumstances, without making people feel that they are forced to go on a trek which they are not capable of, or deprived of journeys that they want to go on. Using a base camp is a fine alternative for first-timers on long tours, as it will break them in gently to carrying heavy backpacks, give them good training in winter camping, and allow them to choose between many different kinds of shorter ski tours.

As with every activity in the natural environment, you should remember to tidy up the area of a base camp before leaving it. Take all rubbish with you, and make sure that the waste from the latrine you have been using is properly buried.

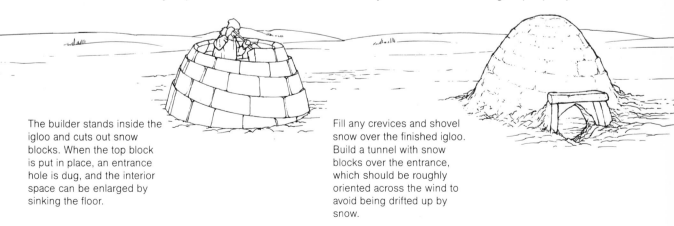

The builder stands inside the igloo and cuts out snow blocks. When the top block is put in place, an entrance hole is dug, and the interior space can be enlarged by sinking the floor.

Fill any crevices and shovel snow over the finished igloo. Build a tunnel with snow blocks over the entrance, which should be roughly oriented across the wind to avoid being drifted up by snow.

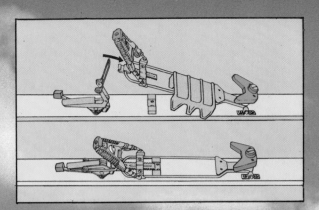

Haute-route bindings enable you to lift your heel from the ski when going up a mountain, but they can be locked so that the heel is held against the ski when you go downhill. The bindings at the left are equipped with blades which grip well on very hard or icy snow.

110

Ski mountaineering: haute-route

Climbing mountains in the winter has long been of interest in the Alps and in Scandinavia. But this form of skiing was made less attractive for many years by the development of Alpine skiing and of mechanical aids—such as lifts and snow vehicles—to get skiers up the slopes. Today, modern skiing techniques, especially for downhill, and more specialized equipment have rendered touring in the high mountains on Alpine skis more popular again, in both Europe and North America. It requires excellent fitness, good general skills on cross-country as well as downhill skis, and familiarity with outdoor life and the various perils of the mountains, including sudden changes in weather, avalanches, and glaciers.

Specially constructed ski-mountaineering equipment consists, to begin with, of ski bindings. These combine the safety features of the Alpine binding, for falls, with the mobility of touring and cross-country models, particularly for moving uphill. A simple adjustment adapts the binding to such different requirements. As a further aid for climbing, or when the snow is very hard, special blades ("Harscheisen" in German) can be attached to the bindings to improve grip. Adaptable bindings work best in conjunction with stout Alpine ski boots having comparatively stiff, strong soles. Molded rubber soles (Vibram) give more secure footholds when you must negotiate steep slopes with your skis off, for example in climbing a summit that would be too steep for skis or is bare of snow. The boot itself should be strong enough to give lateral support for comfortable downhill skiing, and preferably not too high or too sharply angled forward. A moderate pattern of downhill ski boot could be used. Blocks that can be placed under the heels to reduce the strain on the tendons may be useful for very steep ascents.

Mountaineering skis are fitted with "climbing skins" of mohair or a velvety material, which are stretched over or glued onto the ski. This is an old idea in a new form: a simple and convenient way of facilitating climbing on synthetic-coated skis that would otherwise backslip too much. Having ascended, you take the skins off, dry them, roll them up, and put them in your backpack. Mountaineering skis resemble short, downhill models—medium or "soft" skis, 160–200 cm (5–6.5 ft) in length. They are somewhat broader than usual, and their front and tail sections are soft-flexed for easier turning. A hole is often bored in the shovel for attachment of a rope or snap-hook if you need to hoist or lower the skis on a steep slope. Sometimes a groove is cut in the tail to take the straps of the "climbing skin".

When ski mountaineering, it is important to choose as good and safe a route for the ascent as for the downhill run. Many skiers regard the downhill run as the real object of the tour, but this should not be an end in itself. Look for a good route down while you are on the way up. Study the snow conditions and consider alternative routes. Climb steadily and methodically, resting when necessary, and do not forget to eat and drink. You should have enough strength left for the descent, and as a reserve to cope with any detours or changes in route. Ski in a controlled "defensive" way, letting your sound judgement determine the route. Your personal gear must be augmented, for any high-mountain touring, by Alpine equipment such as climbing ropes, an ice axe, crampons, and safety items.

Summary

The following list of essential tasks will remind you of what should be done to ensure the success of your ski tours.

Preparations: Careful planning is needed, taking into account the fitness and skiing experience of the participants. Choose a suitable area and study the maps. Discuss the choice of route, halting places, and alternatives for overnighting. See that all information about paths and cabins is up-to-date. Decide together on proper equipment for individuals and for the group. Appoint the people responsible for particular tasks, and select a leader.

Safety: The strength or weakness of the group depends on its combined skill and experience. Everyone should know his weak points as well as his abilities. Remember that an injury or infection can alter any plans drastically. Always leave yourself a good margin against mishaps, and take safety equipment with you for the whole group.

Planning: The degree of difficulty of your tour should be decided with regard to the capacity of the participants. Take into account the snow conditions, terrain, and time of year. Alternate long, strenuous stages with easy ones. Allow rest days, and spare days, on longer tours—and plan for alternative routes and overnighting places in case your circumstances change. Always leave a note of your intended route with the local snow ranger or ski-patrol leader for the area, and follow that route if possible.

Packs and equipment: Equipment is as good as the skill and experience of the person using it. Try to find equipment that can be utilized in more than one way, or can be combined with—or complement—other equipment. Improve your own equipment by shaping and adapting it to particular needs. You can often manage with the simplest tools, and a heavy pack is a safety risk in itself. Keep your equipment in good order, checking its condition and repairing any damage. Arrange your pack so that you know where everything is and can reach it easily, even when the external conditions are difficult.

Daily rhythm and movement: It is best to make use of the daylight hours and, therefore, to start early. About two hours will be needed between waking up and starting off with the whole group. A small group moves more quickly and regularly than a larger one. A calm, even rate of effort, with brief halts at intervals, is advisable: usually you ski for 40–45 minutes, then rest for 5–15 minutes. Take into account how intensive your exertions will be, and try to cover the more arduous parts of the day's journey during the early stages. Plan for a generous lunch break in the middle of the day with an opportunity to eat, drink, and rest.

Do not make your daily stages too long. In mountainous terrain, about 12–20 km (7–12 miles) is reasonable. You should only ski more than 25 km (15 miles) a day if the conditions are very good and the group is quite practiced. There must be every chance to enjoy the experience, so do not let your tour turn into a performance test. Moreover, it is better to reach your destination early in the day, not late in the evening. Plan to complete your digging and shelter-making in good time. Under normal conditions during a journey, you will move at about 3–5 km/h (2–3 mph), including short stops for rest. With great differences in altitude, you should allow another 30 minutes for every 100 m (110 yds) of ascent. In steep terrain, even skiing downhill with a pack can be difficult and time-consuming.

Rests: Stopping to rest is an important part of the ski tour, and is often a precondition for being able to carry it out. Choose natural features that offer shelter, or build what you need with snow blocks. Use a bivouac sack, put on extra clothing, and have a nice snack or meal. Decide how long you are going to halt, and lay your backpack aside in order to make the most of this interval. See that everyone rests and that the length of the break is counted from the time when the last person arrives at the spot.

Camping places: When you reach the place where you have planned to spend a night, encourage everyone to share in the various tasks. Each person should be busy and lend a hand with the group equipment as well as individual gear. Involve even the tired members of the group in simple activities. Dig your shelter, pitch a tent, or move into the cabin. Melt snow for drinking and cooking, and ensure that there is enough fuel for the night if you can light a fire. Change into dry clothes, and eat properly in a relaxed atmosphere. Drink plenty and remember your need for carbohydrates. Discuss the events and experiences of the day together. Check the equipment and prepare for the next day by studying the maps and judging the weather situation. Keep in mind that the weather may deteriorate, and have all the equipment assembled under shelter, arranged so that you do not need to start the following day by creeping outside for

something you require. Tend to any small injuries or irritations, and be careful of personal hygiene. Decide the locations of the toilet facilities and of a place to get snow for cooking. Finally, leave your campsite with as little trace of your presence as possible, and a cabin in the same condition that you would wish to find there on arrival.

Touring with children
As these practices show, ski touring is a very suitable pastime for the entire family. You can take along even quite young children in a sled, a traditional means of winter transport. A great deal of equipment may be carried in a flat or boat-shaped sled, like the ancient *pulka* of Lapland. Originally made of wood, but also of fiberglass nowadays, it can be pulled by means of a pole— bamboo is best—and a harness. With insulation against the cold in the bottom of such a sled, the children may accompany you on ski tours and still sleep soundly. Tuck them up properly and be on your guard against the chilling effect of wind on their unprotected faces.

A child three or four years old, once used to skis and to the winter environment, is perfectly capable of skiing along on an outing of 2–3 km (1–2 miles) with the rest of the family. Naturally, the child must set the pace, and full consideration should be given to his or her needs during the outing, which must be over easy terrain.

The child should have proper equipment in order to enjoy a ski tour as much as possible. Warm clothing that does not hinder natural movements and can be easily opened, taken off, or put on is very important. Long scarves may get in the way of ski poles, but keep the children warm during a rest. Fasten the child's scarf securely, so that it does not become loose during skiing. Mittens should have long shanks that reach up the arm to protect the wrist from cold, and they should be of a material which the snow does not stick to. Feet must also be kept warm, and ski boots and bindings should fit well. A clamp or pin binding to fit boot size 10 (Nordic Norm 71 mm narrow) is the smallest size available. Skis for children should not be too long, as they may then be difficult to maneuver. Waxing is essential, since children cannot force the skis onto the snow in order to get a good grip. Waxless skis with patterns or mohair strips are often a fine alternative.

When on an outing with small children, remember that their ability to concentrate is fairly limited. If their interest flags, you should be able to remove their skis easily and play with them for a while in other ways. Their first outing must be relatively short, with as much fun as possible, so that they get a positive impression of ski tours. Do not allow them to become tired of skiing, and keep them occupied by pointing out things of interest in the nature around them, such as animals and plants. Children appreciate the small details in nature and are not so interested in magnificent views or the beauty of the winter environment, although in time they will recognize these as well.

A small, active youngster will use up a lot of energy when out skiing, so a regular replenishment of fuel is important. Snacks of chocolate and raisins should be provided before the child begins to tire. The cold will make children apathetic as well, and you must not wait for them to tell you that they are suffering from the cold. Keep an eye on them all the time and check that their alertness and mobility are not flagging. Take rest stops regularly and let the children help with preparing a snow shelter, digging a trench, setting up a bivouac bag, and so on.

Another thing to keep in mind, when you are out with small children on a machine-prepared cross-country trail, is that the tracks on such a trail are made to suit adults and, therefore, are much too wide for the children, who will find it needlessly difficult to ski in them. You should then go ahead of the children and make your own, narrower set of tracks for them to follow.

Orienteering **5**

Using a map and compass in the countryside is easy for the seasoned outdoor person, but for many others it seems a terrifying task. In principle, finding your way with such devices is no more difficult than following a street plan in a big city. It is simply a matter of starting in the right place and in the right direction, and always keeping a check on where you are as you continue toward a destination.

Equipment for orienteering

When you plan a ski tour, regardless of whether it is a short excursion through the woods or a long journey up in the mountains, you need information on the kind of terrain you will encounter. You may be able to get this information from someone who has already done that particular tour. This is a good method, especially if the information is detailed and up-to-date. But in order to supplement it, you also need some special aids and must know how to use them.

Maps

The most important aid to ski orienteering is a map. It can be said to reproduce the real terrain with a degree of accuracy that depends on which scale it uses and on how detailed it is. Most maps for orienteering are based upon aerial photographs taken from high altitude in clear weather. As a result, they are quite perfect in the rendering of mountainous areas and similarly open land which is not covered by forests or other thick vegetation. It is much harder, though, for the cartographer to give full and correct detail if the ground is densely wooded. For this kind of area, a map must be completed by means of accurate studies on the ground if it is to be fully reliable. Such sources are worth noting when you select a map.

Maps for ski tours and hiking are usually drawn to a metric scale of 1:100,000, but a scale of 1:50,000 is also employed for greater accuracy when possible. Real orienteering maps of smaller areas, which may be of interest for day tours, can have a scale of 1:20,000 and are full of very exact detail. These photogrammetrically reproduced maps are often overprinted with trails, paths, and cabins of particular importance to skiers, in order to adapt them for touring. You should carefully learn all the symbols used on

The three small illustrations show what you can actually see from various points in the terrain, and how it looks on the map.

A The river at this point becomes wider and you see

two islands. The ski track leads over the ice. The summit in the background is half-forested and about 250 m (820 ft) high. It falls steeply toward the east with two terraces.

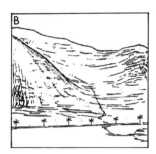

B You see a precipice at the left, and behind it a mountaintop which slopes gradually with a saddle and a lower peak. The ski trail is in the foreground.

C Three ski trails meet at a tourist cabin. In the background is a broad valley bordered by steep slopes. The valley rises toward a peak at 1,291 m (4,235 ft).

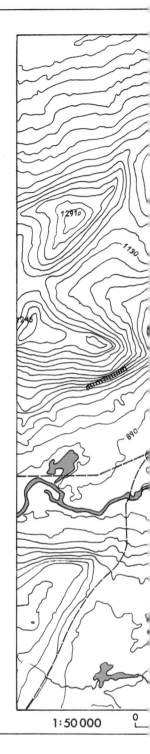

1:50 000

The map tells you how the terrain looks in reality. On this map, the contour lines show mountains and valleys, while the steep slopes are specially marked. In winter, it can be difficult to find small

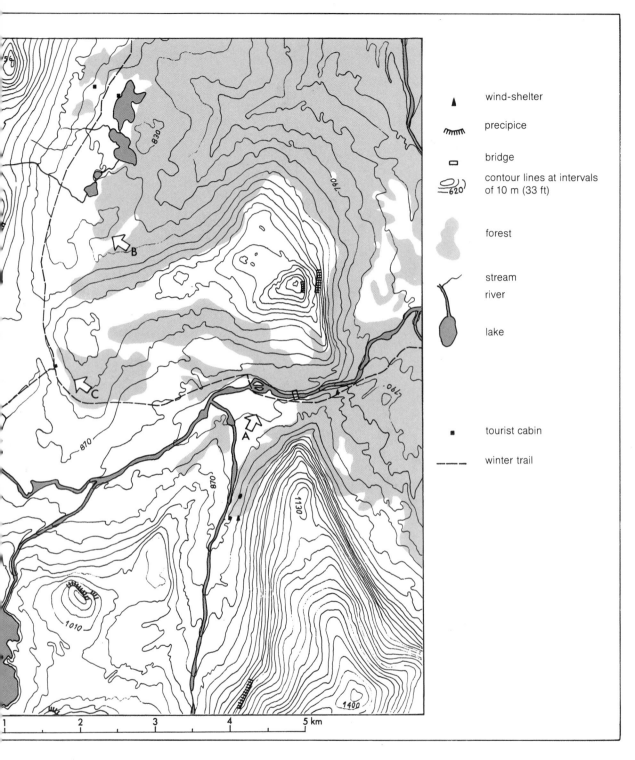

▲	wind-shelter
︢	precipice
▭	bridge
⌣620⌣	contour lines at intervals of 10 m (33 ft)
	forest
	stream river
	lake
▪	tourist cabin
– – –	winter trail

lakes and streams, but larger watercourses are easily located. The borders between bare ground and forests are also indicated. In addition, you can see well-marked winter trails, an overnight cabin, a wind shelter, and many private cabins which are closed to other skiers.

It is generally easy to move across the terrain in winter because the snow cover tends to even out all irregularities. Marshes and watercourses are frozen or iced up, and you can ski over such areas where a long detour would be necessary in the warm seasons. On the other hand, it is very hard to orient yourself exactly in wintertime, since small details are hidden by the snow cover. You must instead depend on the large formations in the terrain when determining your location on a map.

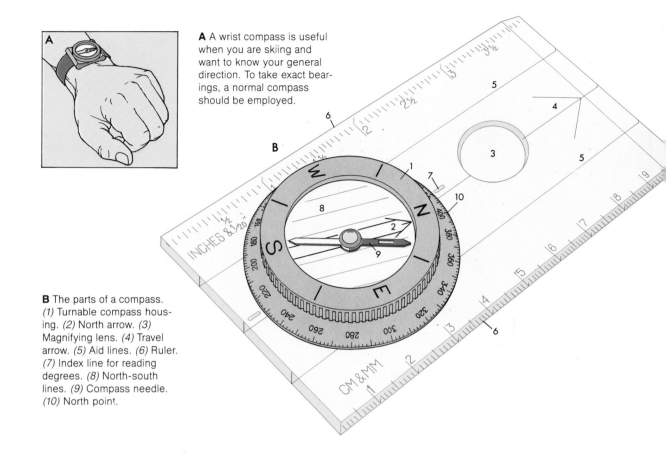

A A wrist compass is useful when you are skiing and want to know your general direction. To take exact bearings, a normal compass should be employed.

B The parts of a compass. *(1)* Turnable compass housing. *(2)* North arrow. *(3)* Magnifying lens. *(4)* Travel arrow. *(5)* Aid lines. *(6)* Ruler. *(7)* Index line for reading degrees. *(8)* North-south lines. *(9)* Compass needle. *(10)* North point.

your maps, so that you can interpret their information completely and with confidence.

When, as part of your many preparations, you set about finding the right map for the area that concerns you, be sure to check its quality. This means seeing when it was printed, and when it was originally made—for the map may have been corrected and revised. Such information is normally printed on the map sheet, where you will also read explanations of the conventional signs and symbols, the compass declination for that area, and so on. Maps of particularly attractive areas for ski touring will show not only paths and overnight cabins, but also wind shelters and places with avalanche risk.

You should regard a map as part of your "capital" outlay and be willing to use it constantly, making your own notes on it and drawing in any additions you find necessary. But be careful not to render any of the small details illegible. The best way to protect a map is to cover it with self-adhesive, transparent plastic. This also protects it from damage by damp, especially if both sides of the sheet are covered. Nowadays, there are also maps printed directly onto laminated paper.

Many people prefer to keep maps in a case with other useful items, which are always easy to reach if you sling the case around your neck. Others fold up the map before the day's touring, put it in a plastic case, and stuff it into a trouser or breast pocket. Both methods are fine, heeding the fact that a map can quickly blow away in rough weather on the mountains. In a group, every member should have a map and learn to use it. Always fold a map so that you can see the whole route for the day, as well as some of the surrounding country.

Compasses
A compass needle always points toward "magnetic north" and thus helps you to find directions. Before comparing it with actual map directions, you should be aware of the various types and functions of compasses for skiing.

Your compass must be shockproof, and housed in a liquid-filled box which serves to check the needle's oscillations quickly. For ski orienteering, the best type is a protractor compass—in the Silva range, for example—with a transparent housing, and with orientation lines

A As a rough way of finding the north-south direction, when the sun is shining, you can use an ordinary wristwatch. Look at the midpoint of the shortest distance between the hour-hand and the number 12 on the watch (it is the number 2 as shown here). Face this point toward the sun. The number 6 will then be facing toward north and the number 12 toward south. This is because the sun moves around the earth half as fast as the hour-hand moves around the watch dial (once every 24 hours as opposed to once every 12 hours), and 12 noon is the local time when the sun is due south.

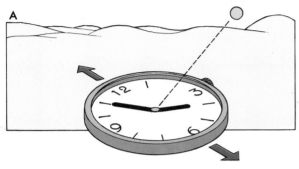

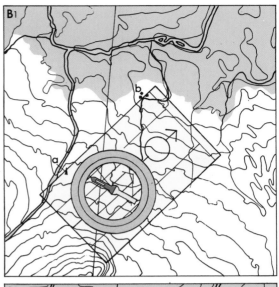

B Charting a course on the map with the help of a compass. You want to know which bearing to take in going from *a* to *b* on the map. *(1)* Lay the compass on the map, with its aid lines or ruler along the desired course. The travel arrow should point toward your destination. *(2)* Turn the compass housing so that the north-south lines are parallel to the meridians on the map. The north point on the compass should lie in the same direction as that on the map.

(3) Hold the compass level in your hand and turn your body until the north (red) end of the compass needle lies directly over that of the north arrow. The travel arrow will now be pointing in the desired direction. Read this bearing in degrees on the index line of the compass. *(4)* If you cannot see your goal in the actual landscape, find another point such as a hilltop and head for it, then take a compass bearing to a further point, and so on until you reach the goal.

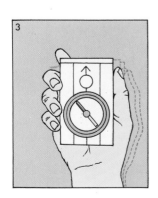

parallel to the north-south line. The compass housing should be mounted on a transparent plastic baseplate, marked along the edge with a rule in centimeters and millimeters, and having a line-of-march or "travel" arrow. It is an advantage if the compass is also fitted with interchangeable scales for different kinds of maps, and with a built-in magnifying lens for small details on a map. The compass housing turns and is marked in 360 degrees, starting with north. East is therefore 90°, south 180°, and west 270°. Of the various new systems that have come into use—although not in Britain—the Scandinavian one divides the compass into 400 "new degrees", giving 100° to each quadrant instead of 90°, and makes calculations easier.

The sighting compass has a lid with a mirror and a sighting notch. This type is specially adapted for determining your position in open country by taking a bearing on distant fixed points such as mountaintops. Another useful aid, particularly in hilly terrain, is a compass with a dipping—or inclination—needle, which is a simple gradient meter for measuring the steepness of a slope. It can be invaluable for judging possible avalanche danger (see Chapter 6). A further type is the wrist compass, which may be very good for holding a course when ski touring, but is small and difficult to employ for more precise compass bearings.

There should be at least two compasses in a ski-touring group. They must be easy to get at, not hidden away in rucksacks. Secure them in place by means of thin nylon or other kinds of cord, so that there is no risk of losing them. In poor visibility, under conditions such as mist or driving snow, and when your view of the terrain is restricted by dense forest, the compass will be an essential aid. You must learn to rely on it, use it correctly, and know that it is always right, even in situations where you are beginning to doubt it.

The whole compass card is divided into four quadrants, each containing 90°, so that half of a quadrant is 45° and one third is 30°. You can rapidly judge any bearing by adding the number of quadrants, multiplied by 90°, to the number of degrees remaining in the last quadrant, when you are counting clockwise around the compass to reach that bearing. This method will also help you to understand the principle of following a course of "so many degrees" with a map and compass, as well as to check that your movements are correct. Moreover, as an excellent complement to your compass work, you should learn to estimate the angles to various landmarks by eye, in relation to a given direction such as the north-south line.

If, for example, you want to travel northwest, this means a course of 3 x 90° (three whole quadrants until west) + 45° (half of the last quadrant between west and north). Your bearing should therefore be 315°. Using the same method, a path leading south-southeast has a compass course of 90° (the first quadrant until east) + 45° (half of the second quadrant between east and south) + 22.5° (a further quarter of the second quadrant, between southeast and south-southeast), giving 157.5°, or 157° 30'. (Each degree may be divided into sixty "minutes" written as 60'.) With practice, you will soon be able to confidently judge the directions of landmarks. Remember that, when the time is noon, the sun lies due south and is at its highest point, whereas the Pole Star lies due north and can be seen at night in the constellation Ursa Minor (Little Bear).

The earth's magnetic north pole lies in the Canadian Arctic, but not at the same place as the geographic North Pole around which the earth turns. This is the main reason why there is usually a difference between the direction in which a compass needle points and the "true north" direction on which maps are based. The difference is termed declination: it may be up to several degrees, either westward or eastward, depending on your location and, to a lesser extent, on the year. The amount of declination is shown on a map for its locality and year of publication, along with advice as to whether you should add or subtract that number of degrees when correcting your compass bearing to get the exact map direction. In northern Europe, declination is not much of a problem, whereas for example in California it is as great as 15° to 20° eastward. Another reason for compass deviations is local magnetic disturbance, as from large deposits of iron ore and from equipment like steel poles, which may turn the needle by many degrees until you move far away.

Watches

An ordinary watch is an important aid to orienteering. It helps you to check on how long you have been travelling, so that you can judge the average speed at which your group has been covering the ground. The best procedure is to build up your experience in diverse situations and learn how long you need to ski a particular distance, taking into account the snow conditions, the weight you are carrying, and the terrain. Keep in mind that the weather can appreciably affect your speed, and may even make it impossible to go on.

Altimeters

A very practical aid, especially when skiing in mountain country, is an altimeter. This is a small, sensitive barometer which reacts to changes in atmospheric pressure. The higher up a mountain you are, the lower the pressure becomes as a rule. At sea level, it is normally about 760 mm (30 in) of mercury, or 1,013 millibar—while at an altitude of 8,000 m (26,250 ft) it is only 540 mm (21 in) of mercury, or 720 millibar. Thus, in poor visibility, you can use an altimeter to orientate by means of the contour lines on the map, in order to find a fixed point such as the top of a pass or a high plateau.

An altimeter must be carefully calibrated to the current atmospheric pressure, which varies from day to day. The simplest method is to adjust the scale when you know exactly where you are and can read your height above sea level on the map. The altimeter can also be used to check the weather situation, which depends on the air masses of high and low pressure that continually move across mountainous areas. If you notice that the indicator on the altimeter moves up during the night, this means a drop in pressure and a risk of worse weather. If the needle falls after a period of bad weather, this indicates a rise in pressure and the weather will probably improve.

Methods of orienteering

You must plan your ski tour at home before you start, using maps and other available information about the choice of route, the lengths of daily stages, and other factors. This will give you a good general picture of what to expect during the actual tour. Similarly, once you have begun the tour, you should plan each day's stage in detail with regard to the general fitness of the participants and the external circumstances, including the snow and weather conditions, which will involve orienteering.

Choosing a route

Consider whether there are marked ski trails in the area, and how they are signposted. The map might give indications of other suitable routes, along natural hollows, frozen streams, or rivers. There may be telephone or power lines crossing the mountains—but although these may represent the shortest and most direct routes, they are not necessarily the best for skiing.

The most important conventional sign on the map is the contour line. This connects all the points on the map which have a particular altitude. The distance between contour lines may vary in altitude from 10 to 25 m (33 to 82 ft) on a map used for orienteering. The smaller the distance between the contour lines employed in making the map, the greater is the accuracy with which the variations of height are rendered. Study the contour lines carefully until you can visualize the high ground rising toward you from the map and the hollows sinking away from you. If you are uncertain, look at the streams and watercourses, which always flow downhill and often end in lakes or ponds.

Finding the most convenient route is generally a matter of avoiding large variations in height. It is less tiring to ski a slightly longer distance without climbing than to struggle up to high ground and then down the other side. You must also consider alternative routes and possible changes of course. Snow conditions or altered weather may force you to ski a different route from what you originally intended. Further, it can be difficult to find your way in forests because you have no overall view of the country, and it may be best to follow a watercourse or even the shore of a lake. The map will show you if there are open stretches, hollows, or ridges leading in the right direction. Study the map constantly, comparing it with any objects on the ground that you can positively identify, and checking the direction with your compass.

In the mountains, it is easier to see out over the terrain, when the weather is clear and visibility is good. In general, you follow the courses of the valleys and can easily pick up the depressions between mountains which the trails lie along. However, it may be hard in these surroundings to estimate the distance to faraway points. Make use of your watch as you ski, and calculate the distances you cover. You can, in fact, develop your ability to estimate a distance up to several miles. Nevertheless, even when visibility is fine, you should get used to setting a compass course, and it will then become routine to work with map and compass.

An altimeter is basically a graduated barometer which responds to changes in air pressure. (1) Scale marked in thousands of meters above sea level (from 0 to 6 km, or almost 20,000 feet). (2) Scale marked in hundreds of meters above sea level. (3) Barometric scale marked from 705 to 790 millimeters of mercury. (4) Barometric scale marked 625–705 mm. (5) Barometric scale marked 555–625 mm. (6) Indicator. Since the altimeter must be properly calibrated, it is best to adjust the height scale when you know exactly how far above sea level you are. You will then also have obtained the correct air pressure.

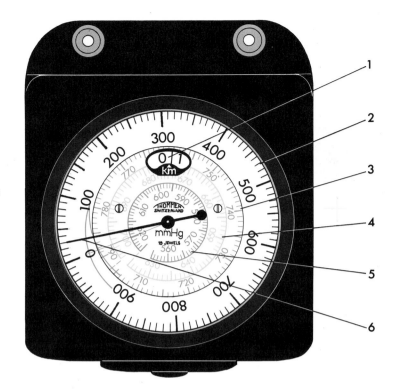

An example of a practical application of the altimeter. You find yourself at a cabin whose altitude is 880 m (2,887 ft) above sea level according to the map. (1) Adjust the height scale to this altitude and read off the air pressure. (2) When you subsequently go up to a mountaintop whose altitude is 1,770 m (5,807 ft), the air pressure decreases and the altimeter indicates the new height, assuming that other conditions have not changed.

When camping out at night, you should note the air pressure as soon as you reach the campsite. If the pressure changes during the night, it shows how the weather will be: worse if the pressure drops, and better if it rises.

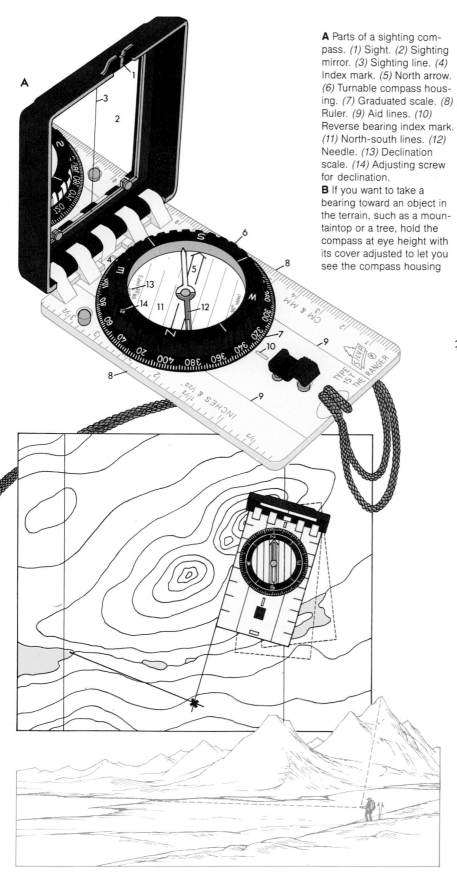

A Parts of a sighting compass. *(1)* Sight. *(2)* Sighting mirror. *(3)* Sighting line. *(4)* Index mark. *(5)* North arrow. *(6)* Turnable compass housing. *(7)* Graduated scale. *(8)* Ruler. *(9)* Aid lines. *(10)* Reverse bearing index mark. *(11)* North-south lines. *(12)* Needle. *(13)* Declination scale. *(14)* Adjusting screw for declination.

B If you want to take a bearing toward an object in the terrain, such as a mountaintop or a tree, hold the compass at eye height with its cover adjusted to let you see the compass housing reflected in the mirror. Turn toward the object so that you can see it through the sight, and make sure that the sighting line intersects the reflections of the index marks. Keep the compass in this position and turn its housing until the north arrow is aligned with the needle, whose north end should be toward the north point on the housing. The object's bearing in degrees can then be read on the scale at the index mark.

Suppose that you do not know exactly where you are on the map, but can use the

map to identify two objects in the terrain: a mountaintop, and a cove in a lake. Your map location can be found by taking a cross-bearing as follows. Hold the compass in front of you so that the travel arrow points toward the mountaintop. Lower your arm without turning the compass, keeping it level. Turn its housing until the north arrow aligns with the north end of the needle. Then place the compass on the map so·that its ruler passes over the position of the mountaintop. Rotate the compass about this position until its north-south lines are parallel with the meridians on the map. Draw a line on the map along the ruler. Now repeat the procedure with the cove as an objective. Your map location is where the two lines intersect.

Taking bearings

Although a map may be quite detailed and show such features as minor heights or the confluences of streams, you may still have difficulty in determining exactly where you are at a given moment. A thick snow cover tends to even out the landscape so that many features disappear. Similarly, it is sometimes hard to know where you are on a wide mountain slope or other open area. One method of finding your exact position is to use your compass to take a bearing.

Look for two easily recognizable points that lie roughly at right angles to each other, in relation to the spot from where you view them. They might be distinctive mountaintops, the lowest points in passes between mountains, and so on. By using your compass—a sighting compass with a mirror is best—to take a bearing on each of the two fixed points in the landscape, you can check where you are. Point the "travel" arrow at one landmark, and then turn the compass housing so that the north-south line corresponds with the compass needle. Read off the number of degrees. Next, take the map and draw a line on it, from the feature which you have sighted and can locate on the map, in the direction indicated by the compass reading. Repeat this procedure with the second feature chosen. If you have been careful, you should be at the place on the map where the two lines intersect. Precision is increased if you pick your two features so that the lines of sight form an angle of about 90°.

Reading the map

If you follow a ski trail indicated by cairns of stones or other markers, you can assume that it represents the best route, where the snow will normally be suitable. To prevent the markers from disappearing beneath the winter snow, they are often placed on small eminences or ridges. It may then be best to ski somewhat to one side of them. Do not let a marked path make you forget the map or lull you into a false sense of security. Follow the route on the map, and use your imagination—you will find this useful if difficult situations arise. Where, for example, could you locate enough snow for digging a shelter? How can you reach shelter most easily if the wind becomes very strong? Is it far to a sheltering forest from where you are? A cabin or other shelter from the wind may exist at the side of the path, offering refuge if the weather suddenly changes and your group cannot make it to the planned overnight shelter.

Ski touring is increasingly popular in North America, where extensive areas for ski rambling in wintertime exist in New York, Vermont, and other northeastern states, as well as in California and the Rocky Mountains. Here is a map from the Roosevelt National Forest in Colorado where tours of varying difficulty can be chosen, depending on the skier's experience and skill. North of Brainard Lake (1) is a fine place for a base camp. The road from a nearby village is closed to winter traffic and, therefore, good for transporting all necessary equipment to the base camp, which makes an excellent starting point for diverse tours in the area.

A You can choose an easy tour of some 10 km (6 miles) total length, with a variation of only 163 m (535 ft) in altitude. The tour passes mostly through forest country. Its goal is Lake Isabelle (2) in a little basin up in the mountains, lying just south of a slope that rises steeply about 270 m (880 ft). On the way there, you pass along the north side of Long Lake (3) and, before seeing the goal, you must climb up a "threshold" of some 70 m (230 ft). The tour takes 4–5 hours, depending on your skiing ability and the duration of rest stops.

B An alternative tour leads along a valley to its far end, where Blue Lake (4) lies below peaks 340–580 m (1,126–1,903 ft) higher. This tour is also 10 km (6 mi) long, but the altitude variation is larger, about 300 m (985 ft). The tour goes through a forest and the timberline passes along the lake's edge. To the north of Blue Lake rises (5) Mount Audubon, 4,030 m (13,223 ft) high. It takes a good five hours to complete the tour.

C If the weather and snow conditions are favorable, you can try to climb Mount Audubon on skis. This is a solid day's tour demanding good ability on skis and fine personal fitness. The total distance is only about 14 km (9 mi) but the difference in height is up to 877 m (2,878 ft). The first 3–4 km (1.8–2.5 mi) lead up through a forest and, after traversing somewhat steeper woodland, you reach the timberline. Then you follow a smoothly rising ridge to a saddle at about 3,828 m (12,560 ft). From there, you turn southsouthwest and climb 200 m (660 ft) to the summit. On your right, the mountain falls sharply to the two Coney lakes, 700 m (2,300 ft) below (6,7), giving a superb view. The whole tour takes around 10 hours including rest stops.

Scale 1:24,000
Contour interval 40 feet

Remember always to orient the map so that its northward direction corresponds to north on the ground. You will soon get used to turning the map around for this purpose. If you are not sure what any of the conventional map signs mean, check the map legend, for otherwise you may miss important information. Keep in mind that, between two contour lines some 20 m (66 ft) apart, there is still room for a sheer drop of 15 m (50 ft), but it will not appear on your map. The closer the contour lines, the steeper the slope. You can also determine a gradient by counting the number of contour lines in a certain distance on the map. For example, on a map with a metric scale of 1:100,000, you could find a slope measuring 4 mm (0.16 in). If this contains 10 contour lines, representing intervals of 20 m (66 ft) in altitude on the ground, you can expect an average drop of 50 m (164 ft) for every 100 m (328 ft) horizontally—which would mean a very steep mountainside, probably with no snow cover.

Poor visibility

It is very difficult to orientate yourself in the mountains when low clouds, mist, or driving snow may be drastically reducing visibility. Even if you are familiar with the locality, finding your way can still become almost impossible. The only procedure is then to know exactly where you are all the time, relying completely on your map and compass. Move carefully and maintain the greatest possible safety margin. If there is a path, you should obviously follow it to begin with. When you have determined the direction, proceed with your compass in hand and make continual checks.

If there is no marked ski path, you may need to move on a zigzag course or a series of doglegs, heading first for the nearest "definite" feature and next for another easily located point, all the while making sure that your original direction is maintained. It is simplest to head for large topographical features, which you can still hit even if you wander a little off course. With some mountain cabins, you may discover that the signposts indicating them are at right angles to the marked path and may lie more than half a mile off it in either direction.

Learn to calculate the distance you cover by counting the number of pole plants, or every other pole plant, over a particular distance such as 100 m (330 ft). Often, this may be the only way of feeling your progress forward when visibility is down to zero. You should practice this in various conditions, even when the weather is bad. Do not reckon on having a very good forward glide in such a situation, but be prepared to "step out" the distance.

Another problem in poor visibility is that the wind and driving snow may make you misjudge the angles of slopes altogether. In a strong following wind, the whirling snow may prevent you from seeing whether you are moving uphill or downhill. You may bounce up a slope and think that you are going downhill. Follow the map properly, read the contour lines, and check by reading your altimeter if necessary. When you plan to ascend or descend a steep slope in bad weather, it is also important that you traverse an equal distance in each direction, so that your original line of travel is not changed. If you are at all uncertain, it is best to try to move straight up or down the fall line on foot, with your skis on your backpack: this is often the only safe way of moving downhill in a strong following wind.

If you get lost

Never take a gamble—pick your way promptly back along your own ski tracks if you are in any doubt. You may find it hard to run into the wind, and your tracks will soon disappear. Seek a sheltered spot, dig a snowhole, and await clearer conditions. Do nothing in too much of a hurry, and avoid giving way to panic. Above all, rely on your compass, and be ready for any chance of taking your bearings.

Put up your bivouac sack, change into dry clothes, eat and drink something hot. See that everyone in the group is kept busy, and discuss the situation objectively. When did you last know precisely where you were? Should you go on, or await better weather? There are no enemies around you to contend with, except your own imagination and fear. If you have prepared yourselves well, and have equipment that is suited to its purpose, you should have no reason for acting rashly.

Before starting a ski tour, or continuing one in bad weather, you must always assess the risks. Never allow yourself to be in such a rush to reach your destination that you cannot lie up in a cabin, or a snow shelter of your own making, to wait for better conditions. Do not needlessly squander your strength, either—you cannot conquer the forces of nature, and must only adapt to them.

Safety **6**

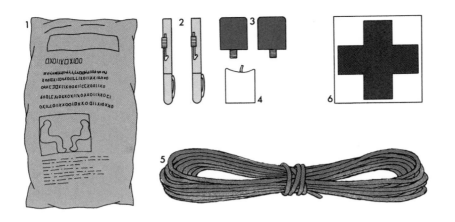

Safety equipment. *(1)* A roomy bivouac sack, at least 2 m (6 ft) long, for two to three people. *(2)* An emergency-rocket pen that can send up smoke or flares *(3)* of various colors—white, green, or red. *(4)* Stearin candles give light and warmth in a snow shelter. *(5)* Safety line made of red nylon, 20 m (66 ft) long, 4 mm (0.16 in) diameter. *(6)* First-aid kit. *(7)* Screwdriver.

Three factors should be working successfully on a ski tour in order to let you experience the greatest possible satisfaction under conditions of maximum safety. These are: the individual, the equipment, and the environment. Your own physical capacity and degree of psychological balance, together with a measure of technical proficiency on skis, will be applied to the forest or mountain environment where you plan to do your ski trekking. Your equipment, besides being matched to your own potential, experience, and skill in handling it, should also be suited to the demands of the natural surroundings. A ski tour that agrees well with your capability and previous experience can reward you with achievements which have not come about by chance—but it is you who create the basis for these.

Principles of safe skiing

You must always act in a responsible way, and be aware of your limitations, *before* an unfamiliar or dangerous situation arises. For example, if you are unsure of the capabilities of yourself or your group, plan a short tour rather than a longer one. Make a prompt assessment of any unexpected circumstances that arise, and be ready to turn back in good time. If the situation renders it useless either to go on or to turn back, then you must decide in advance to bivouac in the snow or to find some other suitable means of shelter.

Never go on long tours alone, whether in forest or in mountain country. Do not use equipment that is inferior, or inadequate for the conditions you may encounter. Always leave a note of your planned movements with someone, such as a ski ranger, or in a place where it will be noticed. Remember to report when you have returned from a tour, so that your note does not set a search operation in motion. Your note should include information such as the number of people with you, the route you intend to take, your destination, and what time you expect to be back. It is also a good idea to state what equipment the group is carrying. If anything should go wrong, a rescue operation can be mounted quickly and the searchers will know where to start looking for you. Thus, it is important that you and your companions stick to your planned itinerary, instead of randomly and thoughtlessly changing routes and destinations.

Do not start your tour if the weather is already bad, or is deteriorating. Adapt the scope and length of your journey to the prevailing weather situation. Never gamble either on the weather or on the route you choose. Pick the safest of the alternatives when you climb a mountain slope and when you ski down it. Choose a different route or turn back if you are at all doubtful. There is never such a hurry that you cannot postpone your departure until the following day, or make a detour of some hours, if this is safer. Do not let a planned journey become an end in itself, or a high mountain peak become a matter of prestige.

High-mountain (haute-route) skiing, and the scaling of summits, should be reserved for days with settled weather. Ski in the forest on a trail you know to be sheltered, if the weather is bad. There is no point in struggling to a mountaintop in a strong wind when the clouds or driving snow promise to prevent the slightest chance of a view over the surrounding country. It is also very dangerous: you can easily make errors of judgement in poor visibility, and perhaps get lost or fall down a steep slope. The mountain will always be there, so wait until a better opportunity for climbing presents itself.

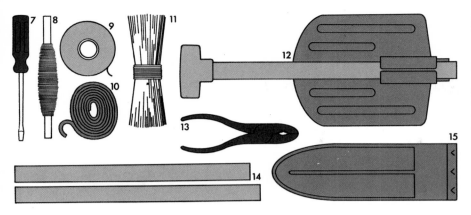

(8) Wire of copper or soft iron. (9) Insulating tape. (10) Strong leather straps. (11) Snow brush for clothes and boots when camping. (12) Small collapsible snow shovel of aluminum. (13) Combination pliers with cutter. (14) PVC plastic tubing of various sizes for repairing poles. (15) Spare ski tip.

Safety equipment

Your greatest assets of sound judgement, skill, and experience should be backed up by certain safety items. All your gear, including clothes, boots, skis, and rucksack, obviously comprises an important part of your total safety insurance. Clothes should be of the right kind in suitable materials, boots must be warm and adequately strong, and skis must be matched to your technique and the terrain. But it is important to supplement these basics with special items that could be decisive if a critical situation arises.

First of all, you should take with you a bivouac sack and a snow shovel. The market offers small, collapsible shovels that do not take up much room in your pack. Your shovel should, however, be constructed strongly enough for digging in hard snow. A nylon cord, 20–30 m (66–100 ft) long, preferably in a bright color, can be used as a safety line to keep a group together in bad weather. Secure the line to the leading and trailing skiers, then pass it loosely through the rucksack frames or shoulder straps of the skiers in the middle. Spare parts for your ski bindings—screws, cables, and clamps—are worth having with you, as is a spare ski tip. For long tours, you may need a small combination tool, with screwdriver, rivets, and copper wire, for simple repair jobs. Leather straps, insulating tape, and a few sections of PVC tubing of suitable diameter for mending broken ski poles, will enable you to see to most repairs.

Safety equipment includes, of course, maps and compasses, and first-aid kits. There are also signal rockets for putting up flares or smoke in various colors to attract attention, as when an air search of an area is being made. Automatic emergency radio transmitters are under development and may become widely available in the future. Walkie-talkie sets are an excellent aid if used correctly and if they have sufficient range. Keep in mind that radios which transmit on high frequencies do not work well in hilly, broken terrain. You must reach a high point in order to use the antenna to best effect, and this may not be the most appropriate action in bad weather with strong winds.

An ordinary small transistor radio is a valuable item on long tours, as it enables you to listen to up-to-date weather reports at regular intervals. A hand mirror can be used for signalling if the sun is out—you may already have one on your sighting compass. In an enforced camp or a wind shelter, it can be pleasant to light a stearin candle, which spreads warmth as well as an agreeable light: the short chubby ones are better than the thin, more common variety. You should always have a knife and matches with you on a tour. Storm matches kept in a waterproof case make it much easier to light a fire or start a spirit stove.

You can never anticipate everything that may happen when you are ski touring. It is to be hoped that you will never need much of the safety equipment described here, but that is no reason for leaving it at home. Make a practice of always having these safety items ready and packed in your rucksack. Check from time to time that everything is in working order and that nothing needs replacing. The day you need to use the equipment, you and your companions will be glad that you have always taken it along.

The safety equipment mentioned here is not especially heavy or bulky. Remember that carrying too much weight can be an added safety risk as this makes it harder for you to reach cover if the need arises. There is often an advantage in having light but fully practical equipment, and thus being able to move swiftly into a safe area.

Correct interpretation of cloud formations can save lives. It is important to learn something about high clouds (cirrus) and low clouds (altocumulus and altostratus). Thin, white, feathery cirrus clouds have upturned tips like those of ski poles. They are a sign that a cold front with low pressure is approaching and will bring bad weather within 12 to 24 hours.

(above left) Cloud layers of altostratus which are becoming denser. The sun is still visible but snow will begin to fall when the clouds thicken further. The weather can get worse rapidly, and especially if the wind grows stronger at the same time.

(below left) Falling snow, and low clouds with their base at an altitude of only 50–1,000 m (160–3,300 ft) above ground, indicate weather unsuitable for touring in high terrain. Visibility is poor there and the wind may be strong. It is better to replan your tour and stay in the valleys.

(left) Wavy clouds of altocumulus, in parallel bands which extend across the sky, often move fast and thicken quickly into cloud layers. They can lead to a rapid change of weather and are indications of sudden cold fronts. These wavy clouds are treacherous since they are sometimes followed by hours of clear weather before the really bad conditions set in.

Getting into a bivouac sack in bad weather. A shelter of snow blocks has been built a little to windward, and a trench has been dug for the skiers' feet. Strong wind can easily tear the bivouac sack out of your hands, so you must keep a good grip on it when drawing it over your head. Once inside the sack, you can put on dry clothes and have some food and drink. By sitting on a sleeping mat and pulling it up behind, you will protect your back from the cold.

Emergency camps

If you have to decide on an emergency camp, it means that you have already made a serious error! At some point earlier, you have taken the wrong option, either in starting out at all, or in going onward. In any conditions, it is better to turn around in time and ski back to the camp or cabin you left in the morning. Do not make matters worse by pressing on with your group to some illusory goal. Act rationally, stop in good time while everyone still has the necessary strength, choose a proper spot, and get everybody to work preparing the emergency

camp. Work calmly and systematically, so that your temporary dwelling is as purposeful and practical as possible. Avoid getting tired and sweaty. Eat something rich in carbohydrate, and prepare hot drinks for everyone if you can.

We have already examined the ways of using a bivouac sack or bivvy bag. When correctly employed, it affords very good shelter, as long as its occupants are suitably clad and have enough extra clothing with them. Many people have spent long periods in bivouac sacks in exposed places and have managed very well. Keep as warm and dry as you can, ration out food and drink, but eat small amounts frequently rather

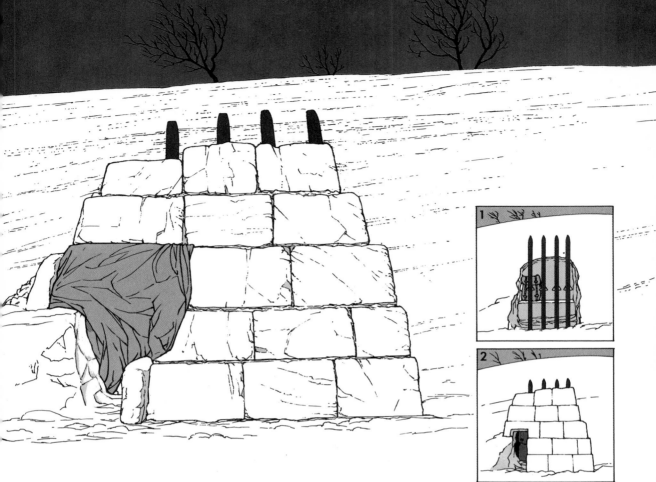

Building a niche. First, choose an adequate snowdrift as near as possible to the trail which you stated in your route plan. While the other skiers dig out the drift, someone must cut snow blocks. These should be taken from above the niche, so that they can easily be slid into place. The niche is formed with a bench along its inner wall, giving about 0.5 m (1.5 ft) per person. (1) Bring in the rucksacks and other equipment. Lean the skis against the drift in front of the niche entrance. (2) The snow blocks should be frozen hard by now and can be stood against the skis until the whole niche is covered. The last person to enter throws loose snow over the blocks. (3) The finished niche. Sleeping mats are drawn up behind your backs. A ski pole keeps the ventilation hole open. Tie a piece of cloth to the pole so that a ski patrol can find you more easily.

than a lot at once. Raise your spirits by telling stories: relate the plot of a recent book or film, or anything to occupy the minds of your companions and guard against worry or panic.

Digging a niche

A type of emergency snow shelter that you can dig out with relative speed is the "niche". You excavate a hollow in a snowdrift so that you get a lengthwise bench for everyone to sit on. Several members of the group can dig at the same time. In principle, the niche can be made as long as you like, and serves to accommodate a large group, providing that the drift is long and deep enough. The hollow should be sufficiently big for everyone to sit comfortably upright, with room for rucksacks. The opening should be no larger than what can be covered by skis stood obliquely on end. Against these, you then pile up snow blocks to cover the whole opening, except for an entrance on one side. Bivouac sacks could be used as a kind of door-curtain or to cover the skis. Shovel soft snow over the whole shelter, mark its position in the drift with ski poles, and perhaps add a brightly colored scarf. Crawl inside, put on extra clothes, and settle in as comfortably as possible. Use sleeping mats for insulation against the snow, and wait for better weather or a rescue team. If you have left a note of your journey with someone, there should be no occasion for anxiety.

Snow pits

If you cannot find a suitable snowdrift, some other form of shelter will have to do. It should, however, be in the forest, behind a large boulder or outcrop, or where some sort of shelter is offered naturally. You can also dig a pit straight down into the snow in a level drift. Make the entrance hole as small as possible, and try to dig yourself in without getting too damp and sweaty. It is hard work digging in a strong wind and in driving snow, so you should try to create some protection for the diggers with backpacks and bivouac sacks. Before starting to dig, test the snow to see if it is deep enough. At least 1.5 m (5 ft) is needed for a tolerable shelter, and 2 m (6–7 ft) would be better. Do not count on being able to build anything above the level of the snow cover, or to cut out neat snow blocks. If you did succeed in shaping a block, the wind and driving snow would soon dispose of it. With a snow pit, you are concerned simply with keeping out the wind and snow and avoiding heat loss, so the entrance must be as small as you can make it. Your elegant snow structures will have to await some other opportunity!

General advice

If you have never been out in really bad weather, it is difficult to imagine how you will react to the roar of the wind in your ears, the driving snow that blinds you, and the insidious feeling of tiredness and paralysis that results from lack of glycogen and chilling of the body. All this acts as a shock to the human system. The best defense is rational and purposeful behavior, which your earlier training should render instinctive. Make use, therefore, of every chance to practice and develop your skill in finding suitable places for digging your own shelter, and to accustom yourself to living in the snow.

Go out a little distance in bad weather, under safe conditions, and try to make an emergency snow shelter. Practice taking out a bivouac sack and getting into it while the wind is blowing at 25 m/sec (90 km/h, or 56 mph). You will gain more from this experience than from all the illustrations and articles that usually provide such information. Practicing in fine weather does not give you the right kind of experience, although it is under these conditions that you should start

Bad weather has struck. Visibility is poor and the wind blows harder. Now the group leader—or, if none was chosen, the most experienced member—must see that the group stays together, and that everybody is occupied if an emergency shelter is to be built. In such a situation, the group is only as strong as its weakest member.

135

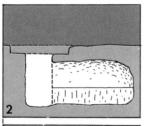

A snow pit is dug when no suitable snowdrift can be found for building a niche. *(1)* Dig the pit straight into the snow at least 1.5 m (5 ft) deep. This is not easy in bad weather as the wind blows snow into the pit, so try to shelter it with your equipment or with snow blocks. *(2)* Form a bench along each side of the pit, while someone prepares several snow blocks about 30 cm (1 ft) thick. *(3)* Lay the skis and poles over the pit to make a roof below the snow level. If necessary, you can dig a small hole 30 cm deep for each end of each ski. The snow blocks are then laid on top and should lie flush with the snow cover: otherwise the wind may gradually sweep them away.

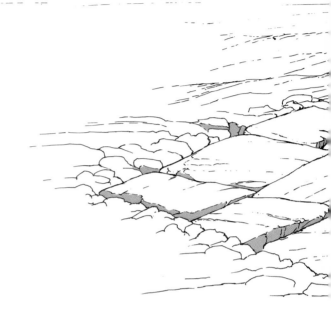

your ski tours and familiarize yourself with both equipment and the environment.

If you lack any extended experience of sheltering in the snow and of skiing in bad weather, it is unlikely that you could manage an emergency camp in a crisis. What must be emphasized once more, then, is the importance of turning back while there is still time, and of never taking needless risks.

Injuries and accidents

When you are ski touring, even an insignificant injury can be a problem for the whole group and, in extreme circumstances, can even become an emergency. The most common minor injuries that occur are sores caused by chafing of the feet or other parts of the body. The latter may occur when your clothes are too tight and perhaps

soiled, or if you are not used to carrying a heavy rucksack. Wash the irritated area clean with soap and water, and smear on a thin layer of some suitable disinfectant skin ointment. Protect the damaged area with a piece of foam rubber, or Elastoplast or another adhesive plaster. Rubbed areas on the feet can create serious difficulties if not attended to in time.

The probable cause of foot trouble is that you are not used to ski boots or have a pair which is not sufficiently worn in. Prevention, or prompt care, is always best. Put in a half-sole and protect the sensitive skin on heels and toes with adhesive plasters. Do this at the very start of your tour, and let them stay in place until you are back home again. Dry, clean stockings and socks will also reduce the risk from the beginning. If you already have some reddening of the skin, or a blister, you should see to it as quickly as possible—even if you have to do it out on the mountainside, in a

everyone—in a group should have had some training in first aid, and should know how to deal with a broken leg, a dislocated shoulder, and similar injuries.

On a long ski tour, it may happen that someone catches cold or another infection that reduces fitness. Remember that any kind of physical exertion is unsuitable for a person with a high temperature or an infection. Rest, and medicine of a simple fever-reducing type, are the best remedies. Cut short your tour and return earlier than planned, bearing in mind that no group is stronger than its weakest link. The group must be united in trying not to aggravate this situation.

Avalanches

Most of us regard snow as something quite harmless: beautiful to see when it falls to the ground in the countless forms of snowflakes, or soft and pleasant to tumble in when skiing. At times, it is a nuisance when you must shovel snow away from the front of your house or garage. Then, too, you realize that snow has a surprising weight on the spade as the temperature rises above freezing and the denser process of thawing begins.

Under certain circumstances, it can be deadly dangerous to venture onto a covering of snow on a slope. One cubic meter (about 35 cubic feet) of new snow weighs between 30 and 60 kg (66 and 132 lb), while the same volume of fine-grained, wind-packed snow can weigh up to 300 kg (660 lb). Damp, coarse snow may weigh from 400 to 600 kg (880 to 1320 lb) per cubic meter. An area 20 m (66 ft) wide and 25 m (82 ft) long, covered to a depth of 20 cm (8 in), contains 100 cubic meters of snow. Depending on the type of snow, therefore, this cover weighs between half a ton and fifty tons—which puts a whole new complexion on it, especially if it starts to slide down a mountainside.

Avalanches are the greatest peril that skiers

bivouac sack. Do not wait until the next halt, as it may then be too late. There is always a risk of an open sore becoming infected and preventing you from continuing as planned.

The importance of skiing in a controlled, "defensive" way, especially downhill in unknown territory, has already been noted. One of the reasons is the obvious risk of falling and sustaining an injury. In a remote area, even a minor injury creates a difficult problem of transportation for the other skiers. As a rule, the most sensible thing to do is arrange some form of shelter and protection for the injured person and see that he or she is warm. Leave at least one person with the casualty in an easily recognizable place, then go for help. Modern snow vehicles, such as "snocats", "skidoos" with sleds, or even helicopters, are the best choice when it comes to transporting an injured skier home. Moreover, at least one person—and preferably

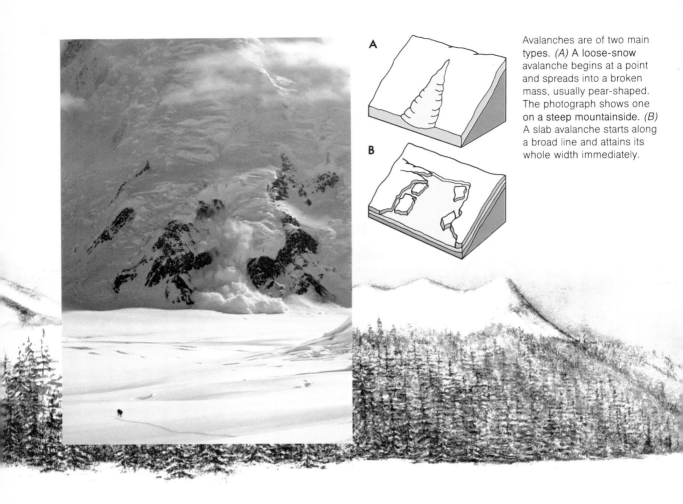

Avalanches are of two main types. *(A)* A loose-snow avalanche begins at a point and spreads into a broken mass, usually pear-shaped. The photograph shows one on a steep mountainside. *(B)* A slab avalanche starts along a broad line and attains its whole width immediately.

can encounter, and claim the largest number of them every winter. Most skiers will themselves have released the slide which engulfs them, and only about 20% of those buried by such masses of snow are rescued alive by an organized search. Of five persons buried by snow, one will die immediately of shock or from mechanical injury. After an hour, there is only about a 40% chance of survival, and this diminishes by half for each hour that passes.

Can avalanches be anticipated and avoided? Most of those who have survived an avalanche accident were taken completely by surprise. They have also been unaware of the danger, and not at all familiar with the sequence of events that lies behind an avalanche. There are two prerequisites for the existence of avalanche danger: sufficiently steep terrain, and a certain mass of snow.

Metamorphism of snow

Snow lying on the ground consists of various layers, with different types of snow crystals in each layer. The differences between layers are produced by factors such as the air temperature, humidity, and wind strength at the time of each snowfall. In addition, snow ages and its crystals change in appearance even on their way down to the ground. First comes a "breakdown" phase, when the hexagonal snow crystals are changed into the rounder, smaller grains of old snow. The snow cover sinks in on itself and becomes more cohesive. This is just a transitional stage, and the snow continues into a phase termed "constructive metamorphism", with cup crystals as the end result. The creation of these is dependent on variations of temperature in the snow cover, with evaporation and new formation of hollow crystals. The snow cover becomes less cohesive and solid, so that spaces and hollows may develop. Sometimes, there can be a "thaw metamorphism" when the snow first melts, and then freezes again, several times in succession. All types of snow can be subjected to the latter process, resulting in the coarse "corn" snow which is solid at temperatures below freezing.

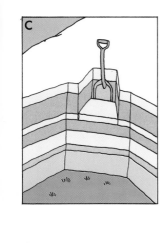

(C) A solidity test will show whether avalanche danger exists on a particular slope. Dig a shaft at right angles to the wind, so big that you can stand and work in it. Cut down into the snow with your spade so that a block is formed. When your spade is parallel to the shaft, a snow block will easily come loose if there is a great danger of avalanche. If you must pry the block loose with your spade, the danger is less.

Illustrated below is the rescue work in progress after a slab avalanche. Those who were not swept away by the snow mass have formed a chain, working at elbow length apart. Their skis are removed and can be used to mark each area searched. All equipment such as rucksacks should be laid aside so that its scent does not spread and hinder a later search by dogs.

These processes of metamorphism, occurring continually in the snow, are not very important if the layers rest on a level surface. On a slope, the snow cover is further affected by its gentle downward movement. You can easily see on the roof of a house that the thick new snow compacts after a few days, through metamorphism of its crystals, but also creeps down toward the eaves so that the cover is thicker there than at the ridge. The different layers of snow move at different speeds, and those nearest to the surface move more quickly than those near the ground. This can cause tensions throughout the whole snow cover—with tensile forces where the slope is convex, and compression where it is concave. There is also tension between the layers. If all the constraining forces in the snow cover balance each other, changes occur slowly and conditions stabilize. But if a sudden change happens, such as a heavy snowfall, a storm, big temperature variations, or even the added weight of a skier, this equilibrium can be upset and the whole slope is set in motion.

Types of avalanches

Two main types of avalanches exist: loose-snow avalanches, and slab avalanches. Both kinds can involve either wet or dry snow, and may bring down just parts of the snow cover or all of it down to the bare ground (in full-depth avalanches). A loose-snow avalanche is characterized by the fact that it starts at a particular point and then spreads out progressively into a pear-shaped course. At the release point, the gradient must be at least 35°. But a slab avalanche has a distinct line of cleavage, through the snow cover at right angles to the surface, and it achieves its full width of front immediately. The unstable layer breaks up and, with the speed of sound, fissures appear all over the surface of the snow, rather as when glass panes crack. The slope is usually at least 25° where the parting occurs. Slab avalanches are undoubtedly the most dangerous type for the skier. Although a slab avalanche can break away along a line hundreds of meters long, and can be several meters high, it is usually small avalanches that kill most skiers.

Snow cornices

A phenomenon often confused with avalanches is the snow cornice. While it may fall onto a slope below and start an avalanche, the cornice itself has distinctive features. Cornices are built up by snow that the wind transports over a mountain crest or another steep place. Large amounts of snow may pile up on a lee side and obscure the point where the actual edge of the crest or ridge lies. Skiers are sometimes deceived into running too near the edge, and must be able to judge a safe distance. The snow of a cornice always breaks away with the smallest possible area of cross-section and at right angles to the surface, so you must know where to ski safely in accordance with this factor as well. Remember, in addition, that a notch or indentation in the ridge can be wholly hidden by a continuous snow cornice, and this may produce unpleasant surprises.

Judging avalanche danger

What is the most practical way of assessing the prevailing avalanche situation in advance? To begin with, the appearance of the terrain is decisive. Most avalanches are set off on slopes between 25° and 50°. If a slope is any steeper than this, the snow will continue to slip off harmlessly. However, a slide may start in a steep sector and travel a long way into a flatter area—in extreme cases, up the slope on the opposite side of a valley.

The location of the slope in relation to how the snow usually falls is also significant. Precipitation often occurs in association with wind, which can deposit large quantities of snow in a short space of time. You should also be aware of the direction of the prevailing winter wind and, in particular, what it was when the most recent snow fell. Even when snow is not falling, the wind can transport large masses of it over considerable distances: this begins at a wind speed of 7–8 m/sec (about 25–29 km/h, or 16–18 mph) and becomes intensive at 12 m/sec (about 43 km/h, or 27 mph). If a wind-driven snow mass builds up on a thin layer of newly fallen loose snow, or on a film of hoarfrost upon old snow cover, then you have a very unstable situation. This condition remains until metamorphism occurs and the snow settles down and stabilizes again.

It is the total amount of snow after a fall that constitutes the loading which can upset the equilibrium throughout the entire snow cover of a slope. The appearance of the terrain is indeed an important factor in making judgements: an uneven, broken-up surface with protruding boulders or trees will bind the snow together better, and inhibit its downward creep. Conversely, a grassy slope or smooth-worn cliff has more difficulty in holding its snow cover. Large temperature variations also affect the situation— cold can hold an avalanche danger in check, and rises in temperature increase the danger. Large amounts of snow usually accumulate in hollows and gullies, and you should therefore avoid these, choosing a route up or down a slope where you judge the snow cover to be thinner.

The most common kind of slab avalanche is characterized by one or more relatively stable layers resting on a cover of stable old snow. Between these upper and lower components is a very thin layer of light corn snow, with its grains held together by tenuous ice bridges. If the load becomes too great, this ice breaks in a chain reaction and the whole layer collapses simultaneously. The upper layer is then subject to increased tension which either leads to the settling of the entire cover, or causes a fissuring and thus a slab avalanche. The collapsed layer then provides a gliding medium between the upper and lower components of the cover. Consequently, it is impossible to judge the real condition of a snow cover without examining the various layers that compose it.

Testing the snow

The simplest way of doing this is to push a probe into the snow. An experienced person will know immediately if there are loose layers in the cover, as the probe will sink in more easily. Another method is to dig a shaft down through the snow to the ground. Choose a suitable small slope and dig your sampling shaft at right angles to the wind direction. Smooth down the snow surface to be examined and inspect the different layers. Look at the shapes of the crystals, the total depth of snow, and the thickness of the layers. Test the hardness of the snow with your hands, fingers, or another object. If you come upon a soft layer, you should carry out a simple test of solidity, to assess the cohesion between the different layers.

Carry out the test on all the layers in the snow cover and check their cohesion. If you discover a weak spot, or suspect one, this is the occasion to remember that conditions can vary and that, because one slope is deemed safe, it does not necessarily mean that all other slopes are safe too. You must dig a new test shaft for each slope.

Keep in mind that conditions change after a few days so that new snow is stabilized and the cohesion between the layers will improve.

Practical advice on avalanches

Always choose a different route if you are even slightly uncertain at any point. No detour is too long if it is a question of avoiding an avalanche. A doubtful area should only be entered in the course of rescue work. Study your maps and avoid snow-covered lee slopes steeper than 25°. Learn to estimate gradients or use a compass that measures angles of inclination. Be particularly alert two or three days after a heavy snowfall, and if a strong wind has been driving the snow about: let the cover stabilize before venturing onto it. Remember that 80% of all avalanches occur during a snowfall or within the next few days. If there has been a recent avalanche in an area, there is every reason to be extra careful. Marked ski paths are reliable in most cases because they follow a safe route across the terrain. Follow wide, U-shaped valleys, or ski along the crests of mountains or slopes that have little snow or are covered with thick, rough forest. Avoid wide, open snow-covered slopes.

What to do if caught

If in spite of all your precautions you get into an area of avalanche risk, you must proceed with the greatest possible caution. Avoid any vigorous turning or breaking movements that increase the load on the snow cover. Remove yourself as quickly as you can from the danger zone by going up or down the fall line, on foot and carrying your skis if necessary. Only one member of a group should venture into the danger area. Keep a distance of at least 50 m (55 yd) between skiers and make sure that you can divest yourself quickly of skis, rucksack, and poles if an avalanche should start. Otherwise, you risk having the equipment drag you down under the snow or injure you in some way.

If an avalanche starts, try to move to the side of its path and grab any available boulder or tree, to stop yourself from being swept further downhill by the slide. Your only other chance would be to shield your chest and respiratory passages by curling up into a ball with your arms in front of your body, and hope not to be buried too deeply in the snow. A red cord, 15–20 m (16–22 yd) long, which the skier ties securely around his waist and tows behind him, may help any subsequent search: part of it should be visible above the snow when the avalanche comes to a stop.

As a fifth of those who are swept away and buried by an avalanche die immediately of suffocation or shock, or by being crushed against an object in their path, your chances of surviving are small from the outset. If you are unconscious, you have more of a chance, since the body's need of oxygen is automatically reduced. A prompt search by companions not carried away or buried may bring you out alive. The time factor is crucial, and only in exceptional circumstances would the most appropriate action be to ski onward for help.

Rescue operations

Most people who have survived after being buried by an avalanche were dug out by their companions. An organized search by the rescue services takes a long time, as these teams must first be assembled and then be transported to the scene of the accident, where they may be in time only for follow-up work and digging out the dead. Nevertheless, the rescue work has to continue until all the missing have been found. There are examples—although rare ones—of people who have survived several hours buried under the snow.

Start your efforts with a preliminary search of the area of the avalanche. Look for skis, poles, and other objects sticking up from the snow. Work upward with 2–3 m (6–10 ft) between the searchers. Use your poles to probe the snow, having first removed the baskets or handles to facilitate this. Always begin at the bottom edge of the area and try to follow the likely course taken by the person who was carried away. The direction of the avalanche usually runs from the point where the victim is caught by the snow toward the place where he disappears. At the bottom of this zone is the point where you have the greatest chance of finding someone. Be particularly careful to search anywhere that the avalanche changed direction or divided, as well as around fixed objects such as rocks and trees where a person could have been caught.

Remember that further slides may occur in the area, and estimate the risk of this before entering an avalanche zone. Place warnings if there is a chance of subsequent falls. If possible, everyone should carry an avalanche safety line during the rescue work.

If the preliminary search does not yield results, a more organized effort must be initiated. Set up a chain of searchers armed with probes or ski poles in the probable area. Always start at the lowest point and mark the area you have searched as you proceed. Work methodically and avoid any haphazard poking about. The most knowledgeable and experienced person should take charge. Working at elbow's length from each other, the whole chain of participants should comb the search area by pushing in the probes in a diamond pattern with the sides about 75 cm (30 in) long. If this is done systematically, you have a chance of 75% to 80% of finding a person down to 2 m (6–7 ft) under the snow within this area. The work is time-consuming and often must be done in difficult terrain, steep and full of blocks of snow of various sizes, and perhaps in bad weather as well. Searching an area of 100 by 100 m (110 by 110 yd) takes 20 men about 4 hours if they work on the basis just described. If they reduce the distance within the probe patterns to 25 cm (10 in), they increase the chance of finding a buried casualty in the same area to almost 100%.

In practice, it has been proved better and quicker to carry out several of the more spaced-out "rough" searches over the same area. But by far the fastest method of finding a person completely buried in the snow is by means of specially trained dogs. Together with their handlers, these dogs systematically work through the area of the avalanche and signal the spots where something or someone is buried. A good dog will search an area of 100 by 100 m in about 10 minutes with an almost 100% success rate. It is important that the search area is left undisturbed for a while so that the dog is not distracted by other scents, such as those which might be produced by your companions' preliminary search. If there is an avalanche dog in your vicinity, this is the surest aid to your rescue efforts, but nevertheless the survivors must still carry out their preliminary search at once.

Another aid now on the market, and in use by people visiting terrain with avalanche danger, is the portable transceiver radio. This sends out a continuous signal on a certain frequency. Anyone not swept away by the avalanche switches his set onto "receive" and, tuned in to the signal, starts to search for the buried transmitter. Such radios require a good deal of training if you are to use them, but they have proved very effective when it comes to a rapid search. Some members of a group should carry transceivers and know how to use them, while also regularly checking that the sets are actually functioning. They can, however, create a false sense of security and it is vital to remember that 20% of all those buried in avalanches die immediately, regardless of rescue efforts and whether or not the skiers involved are carrying transceivers.

Conclusion

It is clear from the above description of rescue work after an avalanche incident that your most important defense lies in anticipating and avoiding avalanches. You should never be tempted to enter an area of avalanche danger, or to underestimate the risks in skiing on snow cover that has not yet stabilized after strong winds and heavy snowfalls. Any detour, however long and laborious, must be worth the extra effort when compared with the dreadful experience of searching for your companions buried beneath the snow, while knowing that the chances of finding anyone alive lessen with every minute that passes.

Famous races 7

Although this book is mainly about the non-competitive aspects of cross-country skiing, the challenge of the marathon has been taken up by many touring skiers, and it is interesting to examine this increasingly popular branch of the sport. In every land with a cross-country tradition, there are ski races arranged by either ski clubs or tourist organizations, for all levels of skiing proficiency. Since the marathons often cover distances of more than 60 km (37 miles), anybody who participates must be very fit and experienced, including practice over the whole distance at least once if possible. A training program for several months should be organized by a trainer or a friend who has skied the course, and should be followed faithfully. Not only fitness but determination is required of whoever plans to finish one of the big races.

In 1978, the arrangers of nine of the major cross-country races met in Uppsala, Sweden, to form Worldloppet, which runs the races as an international ski series. The idea was to give skiers all over the world an opportunity to compete in the world's most famous races—those

Vasaloppet

The oldest of the cross-country marathons, founded in 1922, is Vasaloppet. It is held in Dalecarlia (Dalarna), Sweden, on the first Sunday in March every year, and now attracts over 12,000 starters. Foreigners were excluded until the early 1950s, and women until 1980! The race occurs between Sälen and Mora over a course 89 km (55 miles) long. According to tradition, this follows the route—although in the opposite direction—taken by Gustav Vasa in 1521 when, after an unsuccessful attempt to raise a rebellion against the occupying Danes, he was fleeing to Norway. The men of Dalecarlia, after spurning him, had a change of heart and sent two of their best skiers to catch up with him and bring him back to lead the rebellion. This they did, and Gustav returned to lead the Dalecarlians toward Stockholm. He became Gustav I of the royal house of Vasa. The Vasaloppet commemorates this event every year.

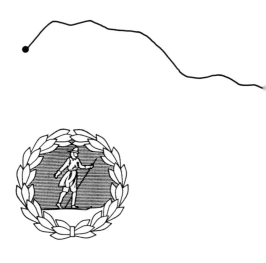

Organizer
Vasaloppet
Vasagatan 17
S-792 00 Mora
Sweden
Telephone: (250) 160 00
Telex: 74244

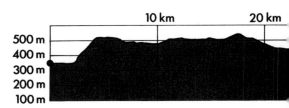

who complete all the Worldloppet races during their lifetime get a Worldloppet medallion—and to give the best skiers an alternative to standard international competitions, especially when they retire from national-team racing. The nine races first represented were Vasaloppet, Sweden; Birkebeiner-Rennet, Norway; American Birkebeiner Race, United States; Rivière Rouge, Canada; Finlandia Hiihto, Finland; Dolomitenlauf, Austria; König Ludwig Lauf, West Germany; Engadin Skimarathon, Switzerland; and Marcialonga, Italy. In 1980, the French Transjurassienne race was added to make the total ten.

There are, of course, other big races which have not been included in this series, such as the Austrian Koasalauf (from Kitzbühel to St. Johann) and the Norwegian Hollmenkollmarsjen, which is more of a mass ski-touring expedition than a race. Skiing organizations in the various countries can give further information about alternative competitions. Here, more details are provided on the races in Worldloppet and some of the other big events, with the names and addresses of the organizers in each case.

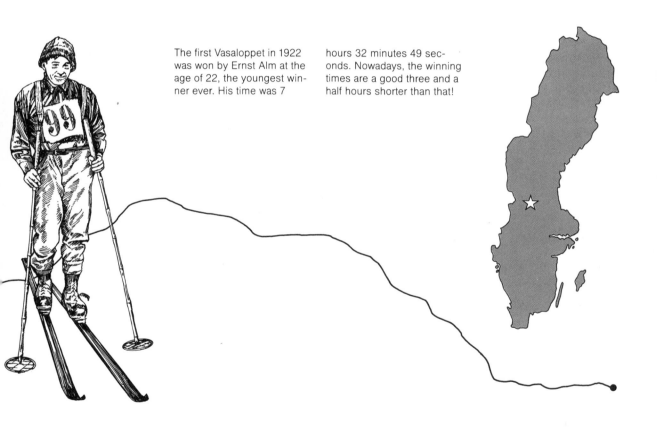

The first Vasaloppet in 1922 was won by Ernst Alm at the age of 22, the youngest winner ever. His time was 7 hours 32 minutes 49 seconds. Nowadays, the winning times are a good three and a half hours shorter than that!

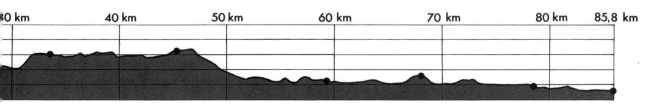

| 0 km | 40 km | 50 km | 60 km | 70 km | 80 km | 85,8 km |

Birkebeiner-Rennet

The second oldest race in the world of cross-country skiing, the Birkebeiner-Rennet is one of the most demanding. To participate in it, you must be a member of a club that is part of a national association which, in turn, is a member of FIS (Fédération Internationale du Ski). Taking place on the third Sunday of March every year over a course 55 km (34 miles) long, this race is unique in the Worldloppet as it is the only one where a rucksack must be carried. According to the regulations, the rucksack must contain sandwiches, a change of vest, socks, sweater, and windbreaker. It is officially recommended that you also have ski wax, snow goggles, and a Thermos of hot drink. Only useful articles may be carried.

Organizer
Secretariat
Kredit Kassen
Postboks 40
2601 Lillehammer
Norway
Telephone: (62) 51660
Telex: 71501

Cross-country skiing is a traditional part of winter life in Norway. Over half of the population is active in this sport. On weekends, the train stations and roads are crowded as large groups head for the wilderness with skis and rucksacks. The biggest cross-country race is the Birkebeiner, shown in the picture at right just after its start. About 5,000 skiers participate in the race. It commemorates a historical event, following the route taken by Norwegian soldiers (who wore birch-bark leggings, or *birkebeiners*) in 1206, when they rescued the two-year-old Prince Haakon Haakonsson.

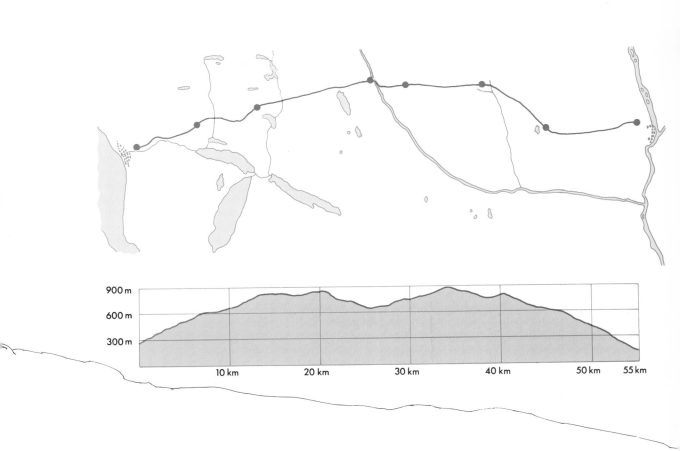

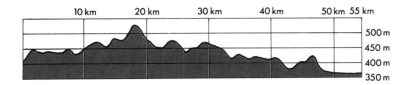

American Birkebeiner Race

This competition takes place in Wisconsin, between Telemark and Hayward, in an area with many people of Norwegian origin. It is the largest cross-country skiing race in North America. Founded in 1973, when 35 skiers started in the actual Birkebeiner and 27 in the Kortelopet (the shorter part of the course), the race now begins with over 8,000 skiers from all across the world. The course, 55 km (34 miles) long and extremely well prepared, runs through ancient American Indian territory. The organizer is the man who was behind the whole Worldloppet idea.

Organizer
Tony Wise
Telemark Lodge
Cable
Wisconsin 54821
United States of America
Telephone: (715) 798 3811
Telex: 4990117

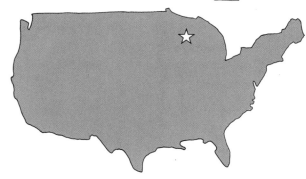

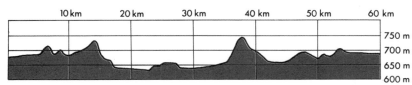

Dolomitenlauf

Over 3,000 skiers are now joining in this race, which was founded in 1970 and begins in the outskirts of the city of Lienz, Austria. The course runs for 60 km (37 miles) along a river valley in the Tyrol region of southeastern Austria, just north of the Italian border, before ending in the town square of Lienz. The Lienz Lauf, covering 25 km (15.5 miles), takes place at the same time, and is meant for ski tourists and families.

Organizer
Langlaufclub Lienz
Postfach 1000
A-9900 Lienz
Austria
Telephone: (4852) 4141
Telex: 4666

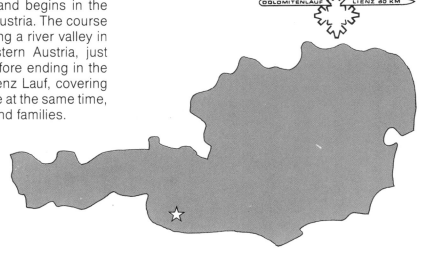

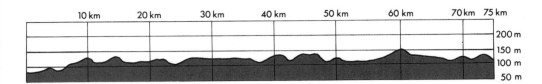

Finlandia Hiihto

This race begins on snow-covered Lake Katuma-järvi at Hämeenlinna. There is no crowding at the starting line as in other places, since the lake is 4 km (2.5 miles) long. The finish, 75 km (47 miles) away, occurs in the ski stadium at Lahti, where a large crowd is always present to welcome the skiers. The course is quite reasonable until the last 12 km (7.5 miles), on which the terrain is tough. The competition was founded in 1974, and over 11,000 skiers now take part. Those who finish are rewarded with a sauna as well as with a medal of participation.

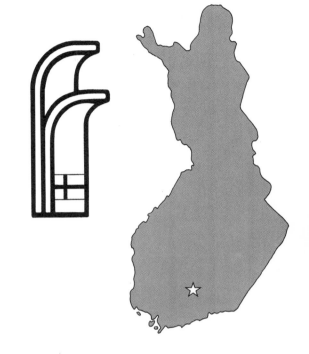

Organizer
Finlandia Hiihto
Hiihtostadion
FIN-15110 Lahti 11
Finland
Telephone: (18) 49811
Telex: 16259

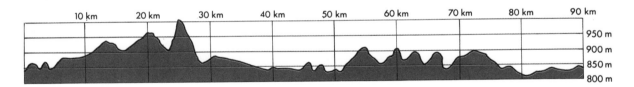

König Ludwig Lauf

This is the longest of the Worldloppet events, running over a course 90 km (56 miles) long. The race starts at the Bavarian village of Ettal, runs round two valleys, and ends at Oberammergau. It is a tough competition with well-prepared tracks. On the way, the skiers pass Linderhof Castle, which was built by the mad King Ludwig in the nineteenth century. Over 3,000 skiers take part in this largest cross-country event in Germany.

Organizer
Organisationskomitee
Auf König Ludwigs Spuren
D-8103 Oberammergau
West Germany
Telephone: (8822) 6566
Telex: 59671

The main part of the field under way at the start of Vasaloppet, the world-famous Swedish ski marathon.

Engadin Skimarathon

Taking place each year on the second Sunday in March, the Engadin Skimarathon is the world's largest cross-country skiing race, with over 12,000 participants—although the Vasaloppet is now approaching this scale as well. The course is 42 km (26 miles) long, and begins on a huge frozen lake at Maloja in the Swiss Alps. It is considered to be the easiest of the Worldloppet courses, being flat for the first 10 km (6 miles) and reaching hills only near the resort town of St. Moritz, before finishing at the village of Zuoz.

Organizer
Organisationskomitee
CH-7504 Pontresina
Switzerland
Telephone: (82) 6 66 85
Telex: 74344

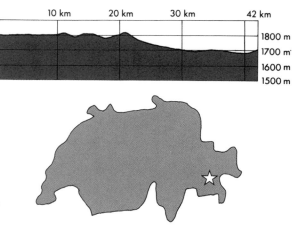

Marcialonga

Founded in 1971, the Marcialonga race attracts over 5,000 competitors to an extremely beautiful course in the heart of the Italian Dolomites. It follows a river through the valleys of Fiemme and Fassa, where the local people turn out in great numbers to encourage the skiers and create an exciting atmosphere. The race starts in Moena and ends in Cavalese, covering 70 km (44 miles).

Organizer
Angelo Corradini
I-38037 Predazzo
Italy
Telephone: (462) 51110
Telex: 400587

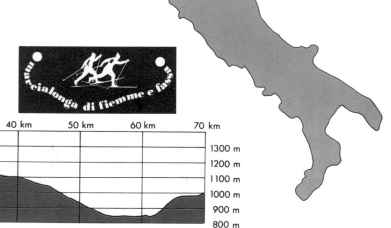

Rivière Rouge

More than 3,000 skiers take part in this race, which was founded in 1977. The present course, inaugurated in 1980, begins and ends at Lachute, located between Ottawa and Montreal. It is 55 km (34 miles) long and is considered to be tough.

Organizer
Canadian Ski Marathon
Box 69, Station A
Ottawa
Ontario
Canada KIN 8V3
Telephone: (613) 236 5830

Transjurassienne

This is the French competition in the Worldloppet, founded in 1979 and already bringing about 3,000 participants each year. As the name implies, it takes place in the Jura Mountains, starting at Combe du Lac, near Lamoura, and finishing at Mouthe. The race is 76 km (47 miles) long, and has the unique feature that part of it runs through another country—across the Swiss frontier into Le Brassus and back again. The course is fairly hilly, and especially tough towards the end.

Organizer
Comité Regional de Ski du Jura
F-39400 Morez
France
Telephone: (84) 51 15 35
Telex: 385368

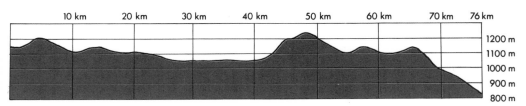

Other ski races

Many additional races exist which attract skiers from all over the world. Below are mentioned only a few that have established themselves as particularly popular events. Indeed, some are hardly considered to be races, but all these events are concerned with getting huge numbers of people out on skis to enjoy themselves.

Canadian Ski Marathon

The longest two-day cross-country skiing event in the world, this is not a race but a tour. Covering a total of 160 km (100 miles), it is divided into ten sections, five being travelled each day. There are various classes, and the most advanced is for those who carry rucksacks of 5 kg (11 pounds) and camp out overnight. Many family groups participate, along with skiers of all ages and abilities.

Organizer
Canadian Ski Marathon
Box 315, Station A
Ottawa
Ontario
Canada KIN 8V3

Mora Vasaloppet

This event, covering 58 km (36 miles), is held in Minnesota, where many Americans of Swedish origin live, and it commemorates the Swedish Vasaloppet. About 3,000 skiers take part every year on a course which is quite flat and runs, like the American Birkebeiner, through ancient Indian country. For those who feel that the distance is too great, Dalaloppet is a shorter version of 32 km (20 miles).

Organizer
Mora Vasaloppet
Box 22
Mora
Minnesota 55051
United States of America
Telephone: (612) 679 2629

Koasalauf

Austria's most popular cross-country skiing race, the Koasalauf, was founded in 1973. It consists of two courses, a run of 72 km (45 miles) from Kitzbühel to St. Johann via Kössen, and a shorter run of 42 km (26 miles) which ends at Kössen while the longer race carries on.

Organizer
OK Koasalauf
A-6380 St. Johann in Tirol
Speckbacherstrasse 11
Austria
Telephone: (5352) 22 18
Telex: 5124117

BIBLIOGRAPHY

Baldwin, Edward R. *The Cross-Country Skiing Handbook* (New York, 1973).

Barnett, Steve. *Cross-Country Downhill* (Seattle, 1979).

Bauer, Erwin. *Cross-Country Skiing and Snowshoeing* (Tulsa, 1975).

Beck, David. *Ski Touring in California* (Mammoth Lakes, 1980).

Brady, Michael. *Nordic Touring and Cross-Country Skiing* (Oslo, 1979).

Caldwell, John. *Cross-Country Skiing Today* (Brattleboro, 1977).

Jahn, Rüdiger, and others. *Skiing Skills* (Tulsa, 1980).

Joubert, Georges. *Teach Yourself to Ski* (Aspen, 1970).

Kemmler, Jürgen, and Vorderwülbecke, Manfred. *The Complete Skiing Handbook* (London, 1979).

McNeish, Cameron. *The Spur Master Guide to Snow Camping* (Bourne End, 1980).

Rees, David. *Cross-Country Skiing* (Radnor, Pa., 1975).

Sanders, R. J. *The Anatomy of Skiing and Powder Skiing* (Denver, 1976).

Schultes, Hermann. *Principles of Modern Ski Design* (Middletown, 1978).

Tejada-Flores, Lito, and Steck, Allen. *Wilderness Skiing* (San Francisco, 1975).

INDEX

A

alcohol 26
Alm, Ernst *145*
altimeter 121 *122* 126
anorak *99* 100
Austria 33 148 *148* 154
avalanches 118 137–141 *138
139*
    rescue operations *139* 141
    142

B

backslip 29 52 53 82
barometric pressure 121 *122*
base camps 109 *124*
baskets, pole *44 45* 46
bindings *38* 39–42 *39 43 84 110*
    111 112
    mounting of 42 *42*
    Adidas Racing Norm 41 *43*
    Bergensdahl 40
    Gresshoppa 47
    Rottefella 40
    Salomon SR Racing 41 *43*
    Villom *39*
bivouac sacks *92 93* 101 102
    128 132 *132*
boots *41* 42–44 *43 98* 112 136

C

cabins and huts 108 109 126
California 120 *124*
calories 16
camping overnight 102–104
Canada 153 *153* 154
candles 88 103 *128* 129
children, equipment for 30 *46*
    47 48 113
    skiing *46 66 87*
    touring *90* 113 114
climbing skins 33 38 41 112
clothes *23* 84 86 97–100 *98
99*
clouds and weather 126 128
    131 134 *135* 136
cold conditions 22 24 96 134
Colorado *124*
compasses 86 118 *118 119* 120
    123 124 126
cooking 88 *88* 89 *89* 92 102 103
cornice 140

D

declination, magnetic 120 *123*
diagonal movement 57–67
    58–62
dogs for rescue work *139* 142

E

emergency measures 126 132
    141
equipment, skiing 27–54 *28–53*
    touring 84–86 88 89 92–94
    96–102 *84–99* 111 112
    (*see also* children, safety)
Eriksen, Marius 40
Eskimos 100 107

F

Finland 54 149 *149*
fires, making 88 89 109
fitness and training 7–26 *17–21*
    56 57 81 82 112
Fjällräven tent *103*
food and drink 16 20 21 24 26
    84 85 86 88 92 *97*
France 153 *153*
frostbite 24 *24*

G

gaiters 44 *99 104*
Germany 149 *149*
gliding snowshoes 36 *37*

gloves and mittens *99* 100 113
goggles 88 *99* 100 146

H

Harscheisen blades 41 *110*
    112
haute-route skiing 38 82 *110*
    111 112 *124* 128
heel locator and support 40 41
    42
high altitudes 25 112 121

I

igloos 107 108 *108 109*
inclination of slopes 120 126
    139–141
injuries and accidents 26 113
    136 137
Italy 152 *152*

K

klister 32 51 *51* 52 *53*
Koch, Bill 33

M

maps 85 86 116 *116 117* 118 *119*
    121 *122–125* 124 126
medicines 25 26 137
mica *33* 34
mohair *32* 33 112
mountaineering: *see* haute-
    route
muscles 8–11 *12* 13–16 *14 15 18
    19* 20–22 *56 57* 60 61 64

N

Nansen, Fritjof 54
New York *124*
niche in snow 133 *133*
Nordenskjöld, A.E. 54
Norheim, Sondre 39 54
Norm, Nordic and Racing *38* 40
    42 *43* 113
Norway 54 146 *146* 147

O

orienteering 115–126 *116–119*
    122–124
oxygen 8–10 *9–11* 13 25 141

P

poles *44* 45 *45* 46 48 57 *107*
    108 133 136 141
probes 46 *95* 104 *107* 140 142

R

races, cross-country ski 54
    143–154
    American Birkebeiner 148
    148
    Birkebeiner 146 *147*
    Canadian Ski Marathon 154
    Dalaloppet 154
    Dolomitenlauf 148 *148*
    Engadin Skimarathon 152
    152
    Finlandia Hiihto 149 *149*
    Hollmenkollmarsjen 145
    Koasalauf 144 154
    Korteloppet 148
    König Ludwig Lauf 149 *149*
    Marcialonga 152 *152*
    Mora Vasaloppet 154
    Olympic 33
    Rivière Rouge 153 *153*
    Transjurassienne 153 *153*
    Vasaloppet 144 145 *145 150*
    154
    Worldloppet 144 145 148

radio equipment 129 142
rambling: *see* touring
reindeer skin 93 101
rest stops 86 89 *92* 100 101 113
Rocky Mts. *124*
routes, choosing 82 86 112 121
    124
rucksacks *84 85* 94 96 *96 97*
    112

S

safety 112 127–142
    equipment 88 *128* 129 *129*
saws 95 104 *104* 105 *108*
Scandinavia 28 33 54 93 109
    111 120 144–149
shelters *100* 104–109
shovels *95 97 104* 106 129 *129*
signal rockets *128* 129
ski, base and edges of 32–35
    32 33
    camber and flex *28* 29 30 *30*
    31 32 68
    geometry *28* 29 32
    manufacture 28 54
    materials 28 32 33 54
    treatment when new *51* 52
ski brakes 41
ski models, Åsnes *37*
    Atomic ACC Spurt *35*
    Atomic Turbostep *33*

Edsbyn *35*
Fischer Crownstep *33*
Fischer Racing SCS *35*
Fischer Tour Extreme *37*
Karhu XCD *37*
Rossignol *32*
Rossignol Randonnée *37*
Skilom *34*
Splitkein Glider *34*
Sundin Trapper *37*
Tegsnäs *37*
Trak Bushwhacker *37*
Trak Triade *33*
ski types, forest 36 *37*
    haute-route *37* 38
    mountain 34 36 *37* 112
    orienteering 35
    racing *28* 30 *34* 35 *35* 36
    roller *17*
    Telemark *37* 38 54 68 79
    touring 32 34 36 *37*
    training *34 35* 36
sleds *90* 96 97 113 137
sleeping bags 92 93 *97* 105 106
sleeping mats 93 *97* 101
smoking 26
snow, types of 48 49 138 140
snow cave 106 *106* 107 *107*
snowhole *104* 105 *105* 106
snow pit 134 *136*
snowplow 68 *68* 74 *75*
spare parts *84* 129 *129*
sun and stars *119* 120
Sweden 28 54 144 *145 150*
Switzerland 152 *152* 153

T

technique 55–82 *56–81*
    balancing 57 *58* 73
    diagonal, two-beat 60 *60* 61
    67 *67* 70 *70*
    diagonal, four-beat *62* 63
    downhill 69 *69* 70 82
    gliding 56 57 *57 58 64* 65 *65*
    overcoming humps 70 *70* 71
    poling *56 57 60* 64 65 *64–66*
    82
    stopping 68 *68* 81
    traversing 68 *70 76 77* 82
    uphill 66 *66 67* 82
    (*see also* turns)
tents 102 *102* 103 *103*
Thermos flask 21 *84* 86 88 *97*
    104
toilet facilities 109 113
touring 83–114
    short 84 *87*
    day 85 *85* 86
    longer day *84* 86 88 89 *124*
    long 92–94 *95 96*–101 128
tracking groove 32 *51 53*
trails for training *71* 81 82
turns 72–81
    basic 74 *76 77*
    inner-edge 74 *74* 81
    kick *58* 82
    parallel *80* 81
    pivot *59*
    skating *72* 73

snowplow 68 74 *75*
stem 74 *76 77*
step 72 *72* 73
Telemark 54 79 *79*

U

ultraviolet light 25
United States *124* 148 *148* 154

V

vehicles, snow 111 137
Vermont *124*

W

waist pouch *85* 86
watch, use of *119* 120 121
wax and waxing 29 30 32 33
    48–53 *48–53 85* 97
wind-shelter *92 100* 101 103
    117 132
wind strength *24* 140

This book is printed in offset by Aarhuus Stiftsbogtrykkerie, Denmark, in 1982. The text is composed by Bokstaven AB, Gothenburg, in 10/11 Helvetica, with captions in 8/9 Helvetica. Photograph reproduction is by Offset-Kopio, Helsingfors, other color reproduction by Reproman, Gothenburg, line reproduction by Kvalité-Kliché, Gothenburg.